STUDENT'S BOOK
with Interactive eBook

2

CEFR
B1

TH!NK

SECOND EDITION

Herbert Puchta,
Jeff Stranks &
Peter Lewis-Jones

CAMBRIDGE
UNIVERSITY PRESS

CONTENTS

WELCOME

A GETTING TO KNOW YOU

Introducing yourself

1 Read the email quickly. Write the names under the photos.

A

____

B

____

Alex
alex@mymail.com

Hi Patricia!

Hi Patricia,
My name's Alex and I'd like to be your e-pen pal.
I got your name and email address from my teacher, Mr Goodall. He lived in Peru for three years, and he's a good friend of your father's.
So, what would you like to know about me? I'm 15 years old. I live in a small house in Birmingham with my mum and my two little brothers. They're OK, but they can be annoying sometimes. I go to Ashton High School. I quite like school, but my teachers always give us too much homework. I usually do it when I get home from school, but I'm not doing that today – that's because I'm writing to you!
I like listening to music and playing games on the computer. I also like playing the guitar. I play in a band with some of my friends. I like sport, too. I play basketball and tennis. I'm in the school basketball team. We usually play matches on Sunday mornings. That's a bit of a problem because I don't really like getting up early at the weekend.
But what about you? I hope you'll want to write to me. There are lots of questions I want to ask you. Things like: what's life like in Peru? Do you like your school? What's it like? What's the weather like in Lima? Have you got a big family? All that sort of stuff to help me get to know you. Mr Goodall says you like volleyball, but that's all I know about you.
So please email me. I'd love to have a Peruvian friend.
Best,
Alex

2 Read the email and complete the information about Alex.

Name	0 *Alex*	Hometown	1 ______
Age	2 ______	Family	3 ______
Likes	4 ______		
Dislikes	5 ______		

Asking questions

3 Match the questions with the answers to make mini-dialogues.

1 What do you do? ☐
2 What are you doing? ☐
3 What do you like doing? ☐
4 Do you like studying English? ☐
5 Where are you from? ☐
6 Are you 14? ☐

a I'm watching TV.
b Yes, it's great.
c I'm from Italy.
d I'm a student.
e No, I'm 13.
f I love playing video games.

4 SPEAKING Work in pairs. Ask and answer the questions in Exercise 3. Give answers that are true for you.

5 Look at these sentences. Choose the next line for each of the mini-dialogues in Exercise 3.

1 What's your teacher's name?
2 Do you live in Rome?
3 What school do you go to?
4 When is your birthday?
5 Would you like to go out and do something with me?
6 Me, too. Do you want to come over and play the new Minecraft game?

6 SPEAKING Work in pairs. Think of an answer to each question from Exercise 5. Then practise your full dialogues.

What do you do?
I'm a student.
What school do you go to?
Chester High School.

Cape Town

London

Paris

New York

Seville

The weather

7 What kind of weather do you love, like or hate? Draw a 😀, 🙂 or a ☹️ next to each one.

◯	sunny	☐	◯	wet	☐	◯	cloudy	☐
◯	warm	☐	◯	cold	☐	◯	windy	☐
◯	humid	☐	◯	rainy	☐	◯	dry	☐
◯	freezing	☐	◯	hot	☐	◯	foggy	☐

8 **SPEAKING** Work in pairs. Tell your partner.

I love rainy weather.

9 **W.01** Listen to the weather forecast for the UK. Tick (✓) the weather words in Exercise 7 that you hear.

10 **W.01** Listen again. What is the weather going to be like in Manchester, Birmingham and London?

11 **SPEAKING** Work in pairs. Look at the pictures. Ask and answer questions.

What's the weather like in New York?

It's freezing!

Families

12 Look at the family words. Complete the pairs.

1 mother and ______
2 brother and ______
3 aunt and ______
4 grandma and ______
5 husband and ______
6 niece and ______

13 **W.02** Listen to Alex talking to Patricia on Skype. How are these people related to Alex?

1 Peter ________
2 Lawrence ________
3 Lynne ________
4 Steve ________
5 Tony ________
6 Mary ________
7 Hemi ________
8 Claire ________
9 Becca ________
10 Harry ________

14 **SPEAKING** Work in pairs. Ask each other about your families.

Have you got any cousins?

Yes! I've got ten cousins.

B EXPERIENCES

Meeting people

1 Put the parts of the dialogue in order. Write 1–10 in the boxes.

- [ ] A Really! Where? When?
- [ ] A What book was it?
- [ ] A Did she give you one?
- [1] A Have you ever met a famous person?
- [ ] A Did you say anything to her?
- [ ] B It was my English course book, believe it or not. I had it with me to help me with my English.
- [ ] B Well, I realised that I didn't have my phone with me, so she signed a book that I was carrying.
- [ ] B It was last summer. We were on holiday in LA. We were walking out of a restaurant when she walked in.
- [ ] B Yes, I did. I asked her for a selfie.
- [ ] B Yes, I have. Millie Bobby Brown.

2 W.03 **Listen and check your answers.**

3 SPEAKING **Work with a partner. Practise the conversation. Change names, places and other details.**

4 Find examples of the following tenses in Exercise 1.

1 A past simple positive statement.
2 A past simple negative statement.
3 A past simple question.
4 A past simple short answer.
5 A past continuous statement.
6 A present perfect question with *ever*.
7 A present perfect short answer.

Irregular past participles

5 Write the past participles of these irregular verbs.

1 think	________	7 eat	________
2 drink	________	8 make	________
3 wear	________	9 run	________
4 see	________	10 win	________
5 lose	________	11 read	________
6 hear	________	12 ride	________

6 Complete the questions with past participles from Exercise 5.

0 Who's the most famous person you've ever *seen* ?
1 What's the strangest food you've ever ________ ?
2 What's the best book you've ever ________ ?
3 What's the funniest joke you've ever ________ ?
4 What's the most expensive thing you've ever ________ and never found again?
5 What's the best prize you've ever ________ ?
6 What are the most embarrassing clothes you've ever ________ ?
7 What's the longest phone call you've ever ________ ?
8 What's the longest distance you've ever ________ ?

7 Answer the questions in Exercise 6 with your own information.

The most famous person I've ever seen is Usain Bolt.

8 Work in groups. Each person takes one of the questions from Exercise 6 and thinks of two questions to add.

Who's the most famous person you've ever seen?
Where did you see him/her?
Did you say anything to him/her?

9 Ask the other students in your group your questions.

10 Report back to the class.

The most famous person Giovanni has seen is Usain Bolt. He saw him outside a shop in London. He didn't say anything to him.

Losing things

11 Read Liam's story. What was in the wrong container?

People often complain about airline companies losing their suitcases when they fly. It's never happened to me, but something a lot worse happened to my family recently.

About ten years ago my mum got a job teaching at a university in Thailand. At first she only went for six months, but she really liked it and agreed to stay longer, so we all went to live with her. We had a great time, but last year my parents decided that they wanted to return to the UK. Because we'd been there so long, we had loads of things we wanted to take back with us – all the furniture from our house, in fact.

So Mum and Dad went to a shipping company and arranged to take everything back in one of those big containers that you see on ships. The company packed everything into it: the armchairs and sofas, the TV, wardrobes, desks, even all the rugs and curtains. Our whole house was inside that big green metal box.

We flew back to the UK and waited for the container to arrive. About ten weeks later, we were having breakfast one morning when a big lorry arrived outside our house. On the back was a big green metal box. We were so excited. The men opened the container and started to take out our things. But they weren't our things. The container was full of gym equipment. It was the wrong one. We were so upset. But the story has a happy ending. The men took the container and gym equipment away, and about two months ago our things finally arrived.

12 Read the story again and answer the questions. Use the word in brackets in your answer.

1 When did Liam's mum start her job in Thailand? (ago)
2 When did the family move to Thailand? (later)
3 How long did they stay there? (about)
4 When did they decide to move back to the UK? (last)
5 How long after they got back to the UK did the first container arrive? (about)
6 When did the correct container finally arrive? (ago)

13 WRITING **Write a short story about something you lost. Use these questions to help you.**

- When did it happen?
- What was it?
- Where did you lose it?
- What did you do?
- How did you feel?
- Did you find it? If so, when and where?

Furniture

14 Tick (✓) the items mentioned in the story.

15 SPEAKING **Name the other items. Which of these do you think Liam's parents probably didn't put into the container?**

They probably didn't put the toilet into the container.

16 SPEAKING **Discuss in small groups.**

Your family is moving to the other side of the world. What five items from your bedroom or house do you want to take with you?

C EATING AND DRINKING

Buying and talking about food

1 W.04 **Listen and complete each space with one word.**

Assistant	Morning. Can I help you?
Customer	Yes, please. Um, I want ^{1}______ onions.
Assistant	OK, how ^{2}______ ?
Customer	Two large ones, please. And can I have ^{3}______ mushrooms, too? About half a kilo?
Assistant	OK, sure. Anything else?
Customer	Oh, yes – tomatoes. A ^{4}______ of tomatoes, please. And some chillies.
Assistant	Sorry, we haven't got ^{5}______ chillies today. Maybe try the supermarket across the street.
Customer	OK, thanks.
Assistant	So, ^{6}______ are your tomatoes. Are you making something special tonight?
Customer	Yes, I'm going to make a vegetable curry. I had one in an Indian restaurant last week so I thought I'd try and make one, too.
Assistant	What about lemons? Lemon juice is ^{7}______ good in a curry.
Customer	That's a good ^{8}______ ! But I don't need any. I've ^{9}______ got lemons at home. So, how ^{10}______ is that?
Assistant	Let's see. That's £4.15, ^{11}______ .
Customer	Here you are – £5.
Assistant	And 85p ^{12}______ . Thanks. Enjoy your dinner!

2 Complete each sentence with *some* or *any*. Then match the sentences with the pictures. Write the numbers 1–8.

1 There's ______ butter in the fridge.
2 There are ______ eggs in the kitchen.
3 There aren't ______ olives on the pizza.
4 I'd like ______ of those tomatoes, please.
5 Sorry, there aren't ______ eggs.
6 I'd like ______ water, please.
7 Oh, there isn't ______ milk.
8 No, I don't want ______ orange juice, thanks.

A ☐

✗ E ☐

B ☐

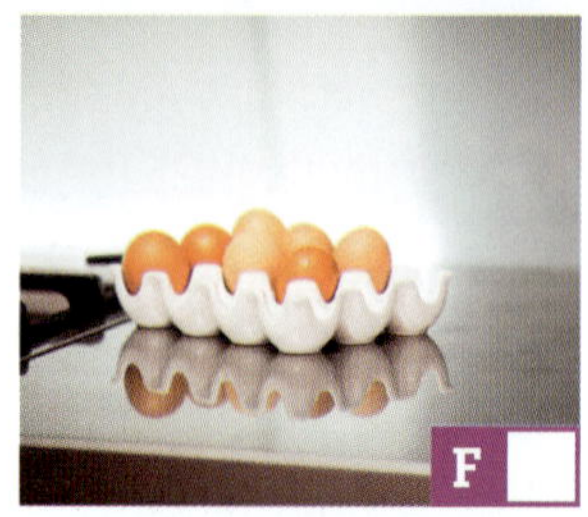
F ☐

✗ C ☐

G ☐

D ☐

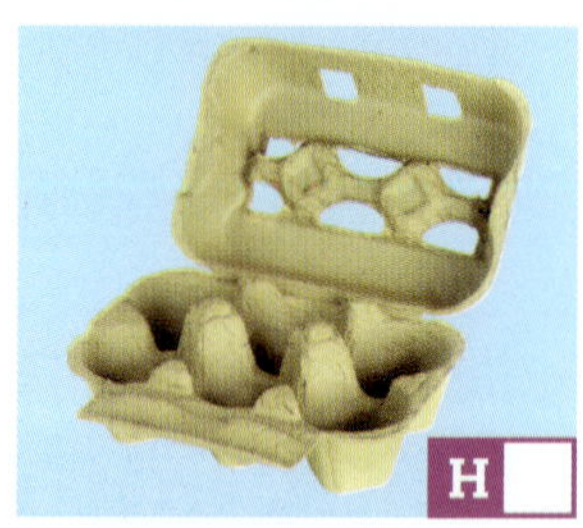
H ☐

3 Which of these things would you always / never / sometimes use to make a sandwich? Write sentences.

butter | bread | cheese | chicken
coffee | eggs | milk | olives | onions
pears | tomatoes | yoghurt

You always use bread to make a sandwich – but you never use ...

4 ROLE PLAY **Work in pairs. Use your sentences from Exercise 3 to do a role play.**

In a restaurant

5 W.05 **Read the sentences. Mark them W (waitress) or C (customer). Listen and check.**

1 Can we see the menu, please? ☐
2 Is everything OK? ☐
3 This soup is too cold! ☐
4 Can we have the bill, please? ☐
5 A table for two? This way, please. ☐
6 We'd like the soup to start. ☐
7 What soup have you got today? ☐
8 Are you ready to order? ☐

6 Complete each phrase with *much* or *many*.

1 too ____________ butter
2 too ____________ onions
3 too ____________ things in your bag
4 too ____________ milk
5 too ____________ noise
6 too ____________ cars

7 Complete the mini-dialogues with a phrase from Exercise 6.

1 A This coffee is horrible.
B I know! There's ______________________ in it.
2 A Ugh! I can't eat this toast.
B I know! There's ______________________ on it.
3 A This salad isn't very good.
B I know! There are ______________________ in it!
4 A This restaurant is horrible. We can't talk.
B I know! There is ______________________ here.
5 A It took me an hour to drive to work today.
B I know! There are ______________________ on our roads.
6 A I can't carry this. It's too heavy.
B There are ______________________ . Take something out of it.

Shops

8 Look at the shops below. What things can you buy in each place? Think of as many things as you can.

coffee shop ☐ phone shop ☐
chemist's ☐ post office ☐
bookshop ☐ supermarket ☐
clothes shop ☐ sports shop ☐

9 W.06 **Listen. Which shop is each person in? Write the number of the dialogue next to the correct shop in Exercise 8. There are three shops you don't need.**

10 W.06 **Listen again. In which shop do you hear these sentences?**

1 You don't have to wait in a queue. ______
2 You have to wear them two or three times. ______
3 You have to fill in this form. ______
4 You don't have to pay for the third one. ______

Things you have to do

11 Read the sentences below. For each one, think of possibilities for a) who said it and b) who to.

1 *You don't have to read it.*
2 *You have to give it to me before the lesson.*
3 *I don't have to do what you say!*
4 *I have to finish this tonight.*
5 *You don't have to throw it away.*
6 *It's fantastic! You have to see it!*

12 SPEAKING **Work in pairs. Choose three of the sentences in Exercise 11. Act out a mini-dialogue for each sentence that you choose.**

This book is really boring.
Well, you don't have to read it.
I do. I have to read it for school.
Oh. When do you need to finish it by?
Tomorrow!

Katy
katy@thinkmail.com

Party

Hi Lucy,

I was really happy to get your text saying that you're coming to visit us at the end of the month. I'm very excited, and you're going to be here at just the right time!

On the 29th our town is having its special weekend gala. There is one every year. What's a gala? Well, it's like a party but with sports and other events, too. There are lots of different activities. We're going to join in, so I hope you're ready for some fun!

It all starts on Saturday. There's an opening ceremony in the morning, and after lunch, there are things for kids – like races and games. And at five o'clock there's a football match – we're playing against a team from another town. Then in the evening, there's dancing in the town square. A famous DJ is playing the music! (I can't say who yet – it's secret!)

On Sunday morning there's a charity run – it's about five kilometres. It starts at the town hall and goes past the school and down the High Street to the park, where it finishes. And guess what? I'm running in the race! (Would you like to run, too? I think we can get you in – let me know ASAP, OK?) And on Sunday afternoon, there's a big street party with games and food. It's going to be great. The only problem is the weather forecast says it's going to rain, so I'm going to wear my raincoat.

We're looking forward to seeing you here. Oh, I almost forgot! On Sunday evening we're having a party at our place for my dad's 50th birthday! We're going to make it a really special party. Please say you don't have to leave on Sunday evening!

Anyway, let me know more about your plans. When are you arriving on Friday?

See you soon,

Katy

D LOOKING AHEAD

Plans and arrangements

1 Read the email. Match the times and the events.

1 Saturday morning ☐
2 Saturday afternoon ☐
3 Saturday evening ☐
4 Sunday morning ☐
5 Sunday afternoon ☐
6 Sunday evening ☐

a sports events
b party for Katy's dad
c opening ceremony
d dancing
e charity run
f street party

2 Read the sentences. What do the underlined verbs express? Write A (arrangement) or I (intention).

1 A famous DJ is playing the music. ☐
2 I'm running in the race. ☐
3 We're going to join in. ☐
4 I'm going to wear my raincoat. ☐
5 We're going to make it a really special party. ☐
6 We're having a party at our place. ☐

3 Find other examples of the present continuous for arrangements in Katy's email.

4 SPEAKING Work in pairs. Ask and answer questions about plans you have for next weekend.

What are you doing on Saturday morning?

I'm going running. / I'm not doing anything.

Sports and sport verbs

5 Complete the table with the sports in the list.

athletics | football | gymnastics | karate
rock climbing | running | skiing | tennis

play	do	go

6 SPEAKING Work in pairs. Which sports do you often / sometimes / never do? Talk to your partner.

I often go running, but I never do karate.

Travel plans

7 W.07 **Put the parts of the dialogue in order. Then listen and check your answers.**

☐ A Great idea. OK, see you soon. We're going to have a lot of fun this weekend!
☐ A Ah, OK. 3.15 is difficult for me. Is it OK if I don't meet you at the station?
☐ A Hey, Connor. What time are you arriving on Saturday?
☐ A Well, sometimes the train's late. If it's late, I'll meet you.
☐ B OK. As soon as the train leaves Liverpool, I'll send you a text message.
☐ B 3.15 – I'm going to catch the two o'clock train from Liverpool.
☐ B I know. It's going to be great!
☐ B Of course. I can walk. No problem.

8 Complete the sentences with the correct form of the verbs in brackets.

1 If I ______ (miss) the bus, I ______ (catch) the next one.
2 If the bus ______ (arrive) late, I ______ (take) a taxi.
3 If there ______ (not be) any taxis, I ______ (walk) to your place.
4 I'll send you a text message when I ______ (get) to the station.
5 As soon as I ______ (get) to your place, we ______ (start) having a good time.
6 If we ______ (not have) a good time, I ______ (not visit) you again!

9 Ellie travelled a lot last year. Complete the sentences with the past simple of the verbs in the list.

catch | drive | fly | miss | ride | ~~take~~

10 Complete the sentences with *be going to* and the verbs in the list.

buy | get up | not visit | take | try | visit

1 We don't like flying so we ____________ a boat.
2 I want to go to Dublin. I ____________ my ticket online.
3 My train leaves at 5.00, so I ____________ very early tomorrow.
4 We'll only be in Madrid for one day, so we ____________ any museums.
5 When we're in Birmingham, we ____________ my cousins.
6 We love Italian food, so we ____________ all the best restaurants in Rome!

11 Imagine you can go on a holiday to wherever you want, any time you want. Make notes about your plans:

- where you're going to go
- where you're going to stay
- how long your holiday is going to be
- what you're going to do
- who you're going to go with
- what you're going to eat
- what time of year you're going to go

12 SPEAKING **Work in pairs. Ask and answer about the holiday you planned in Exercise 11.**

Where are you going to go on holiday?

Thailand. And I'm going to stay in a hotel on the beach.

0 She *took* a taxi in Paris.

1 She ______ the train in Vienna.

2 She ______ to Madrid.

3 She ______ the train in Berlin.

4 She ______ to Rome.

5 She ______ a bike in Athens.

1 INCREDIBLE PEOPLE

Get THINKING

Watch the video and think: what makes people incredible?

OBJECTIVES

FUNCTIONS: talking about things you have and haven't done; offering encouragement

GRAMMAR: present perfect with *just*, *already* and *yet*; present perfect vs. past simple

VOCABULARY: personality adjectives; collocations; phrases with *just*

1

3

2

4

READING

1 Look at the photos. What is your first impression of these people? What adjectives could you use to describe them?

boring | caring | confident | cool | easy-going | friendly | funny | happy | intelligent | serious

2 SPEAKING Discuss the photos in pairs.

He seems friendly.

She looks like a happy person because she's smiling.

3 SPEAKING Use the adjectives in Exercise 1 and other adjectives to describe people you know.

My brother is very easy-going.

He doesn't get angry very often.

4 Quickly read the responses to the survey question on the next page. Who do the respondents admire?

5 1.01 Read and listen to the responses again. Mark the sentences T (true) or F (false).

1 Renata's got a daughter. ______
2 Renata works as a sports trainer. ______
3 Mr Ronay helps children to learn the piano. ______
4 Mr Ronay plays concerts all over the world. ______
5 Deming has never had lessons in painting. ______
6 Deming is very good at drawing pictures. ______
7 Anna's got a problem with her heart. ______
8 Anna never goes to school. ______

6 SPEAKING Work with a partner. Correct the false sentences in Exercise 5.

WHO DO YOU ADMIRE MOST?

1 My cousin Renata is an amazing person. She's 26 and she's got a little girl, Bruna, aged four. Her husband died three years ago, so she is bringing Bruna up on her own. Renata lives in São Paulo, where she works as a teacher. It's hard work, but she's always happy and smiling. Renata's a keen athlete, too – she's a very good runner and she trains a lot. She's already run two half-marathons, but she hasn't won a race yet. She hopes to run a marathon one day. Her life isn't easy, but she always stays **positive** about everything.

Juliana, 17

2 There's an elderly man who lives near us called Mr Ronay. He's very **charming** and I think he's just incredible. He's 85 and he has difficulty walking now, but that doesn't stop him being **active** and doing the thing he loves most: playing the piano. He has always been a very **talented** performer. When he was younger, he played concerts all over the world, but he can't do that any more. Now, he teaches the piano. He gives lessons at home, and he's just started to give free lessons to neighbourhood kids.

Urgun, 16

3 There's a boy at my school called Deming. He's 15 years old and he can be quiet and shy, but he's very interesting when you talk to him. He's also a wonderful artist with an amazing memory – he looks at a building for just a few minutes, then goes away and paints it exactly as it is in real life. He also paints things from his imagination. He's very **creative**. He has never studied art; he just knows how to draw and paint. He's already sold a lot of paintings, and he's just won a place at an art school in Beijing. But he's very **laid-back** about the success he's had.

Li Ju, 16

4 My best friend's sister, Anna, is amazing. She's 13 and she was born with a serious heart problem. She's already had about ten operations, but she is incredibly **brave**. She knows that there will be more operations, but she doesn't complain and always seems so **cheerful**. The problem makes her very weak, so she spends a lot of time in bed or in a wheelchair. But she goes to school when she can, and when she can't go to school, she studies in hospital or at home. She's just had another operation, but she's also just passed all her exams!

Luigi, 15

VOCABULARY
Personality adjectives

7 There are eight words in bold in the texts. Match the words with these meanings. Write the words.

0 is always doing things *active*
1 is usually happy ______
2 is very easy-going ______
3 has very original ideas ______
4 looks for the good in all situations ______
5 is very good at doing something ______
6 doesn't get scared easily ______
7 is very easy to like ______

8 Complete the sentences with the words from Exercise 7.

0 Why are you so *cheerful* today? Have you had some good news?
1 He stood up in the front of the whole school and read out his poem. He was really ______ .
2 She's very ______ and it's easy to see why she's got so many friends.
3 He's so ______ that some people think he's a bit lazy.
4 Have you seen him doing ballet? He really is a ______ dancer.
5 If you want to work in advertising, you need to be ______ and come up with really good ideas.
6 My dad is really ______ around the house. He's always cooking or fixing things or working in the garden.
7 He's had a really difficult life but he's really ______ about the future.

THINK values
Human qualities

9 Think about someone who is not famous but who you think is special.

a Think of three adjectives to describe them.
b Think about why you chose these adjectives. Make notes.

10 SPEAKING Tell your partner about the person you admire.

I really admire my sister. She's really confident in difficult situations.

GRAMMAR
Present perfect with *just*, *already* and *yet*

1 **Complete the sentences with *just*, *already* and *yet*. Then complete the rules.**

1 She's ______ run two half-marathons but she hasn't won a race ______ .
2 She's ______ had another operation.

> **RULE:** In the present perfect, we often use
> - [3]______ in negative sentences and questions to talk about something that hasn't happened but that we expect to happen soon. It comes at the end of the sentence.
> - [4]______ to emphasise that something happened very recently. It goes before the past participle.
> - [5]______ to show that something has been done or finished sooner than expected. It usually goes before the past participle.

2 **Match the pictures and the sentences. Write 1–3 in the boxes.**

1 He's just woken up.
2 He's already got out of bed.
3 He hasn't woken up yet.

3 **Look at Jack's list of things to do for his party. Write sentences with *already* and *yet*.**

1 *He hasn't made the cake yet.*

4 **Use your imagination to answer the questions. Use the present perfect and *just* in each one.**

0 Why is Mum so angry?
Because Dad's just crashed her car.
1 Why is Jacob so sad?
2 Why is your face so dirty?
3 Why is Liam so scared?
4 Why is Dana so excited?
5 Why are you smiling?

5 **Tick (✓) the things you have already done.**

EIGHT THINGS TO DO BEFORE YOU'RE 20:

- ☐ start a vlog
- ☐ meet a famous person
- ☐ travel abroad
- ☐ write a song
- ☐ act on stage
- ☐ learn to play a musical instrument
- ☐ enter a competition
- ☐ climb a mountain

6 SPEAKING **Work in pairs. Ask each other questions.**

Have you started a vlog yet?

Yes, I've already done that. Have you?

No, I haven't done that yet.

→ workbook page 10

LISTENING

7 1.02 **Listen to three people: Jack, Sarah and Ella. They're going to play a game called *I've Never*. Complete the rules they describe.**

Ella It's a game called *I've Never*. So, I think of something that I've [1] ____________________ done but I think both of you have done.

Jack Right.

Ella Then I say [2] ____________________. And you say if you've ever done the thing or not. If [3] ____________________ say 'Yes, I've done that,' then I get [4] ____________________ and another turn. But if [5] ____________________ says 'No, I've never done that,' then I [6] ____________________ a point and it's [7] ____________________.

8 1.03 **Listen to the rest of the conversation and the game. How many points does each person get?**

9 1.03 **Listen again and choose the correct answer A, B or C.**

1 How did Ella's family travel to Spain?

2 What has Ella never worn?

3 What kind of food has Ella never eaten?

4 Who loses a turn of *I've Never* first?

Ella

Jack

Sarah

10 **Work in pairs. Answer the questions.**

1 How do you win a point in the game?
2 When did Sarah travel by plane?
3 Why does Sarah think Ella has eaten Japanese food?
4 Why does Ella say she wants to stop playing the game? Do you think this is the real reason she wants to stop playing?

SPEAKING

11 **Work in small groups. Play *I've Never*.**

OK, I've never travelled outside my country. And you?

I have. / I haven't.

WordWise: Phrases with *just*

12 **Look at the sentences from the unit so far. Choose the correct meaning of *just* in each one.**

1 She's just had another operation. ☐
2 He looks at a building for just a few minutes, then goes away and paints it exactly as it is. ☐
3 I think he's just incredible. ☐

a only
b a short time ago
c really

13 **What does *just* mean in these sentences? Write a, b or c.**

1 Don't be angry. It's just a joke. ☐
2 I've just seen a fantastic film. ☐
3 It's cold today. The weather is just awful. ☐
4 No food, thanks – just a drink. ☐
5 She's just had some bad news. ☐

14 **Match the questions and answers.**

1 How many scoops of ice cream would you like? ☐
2 When did Paula get here? ☐
3 What do you think of Ariana Grande? ☐

a She's just arrived.
b She's just great.
c Just one, please.

→ workbook page 12

READING

1 SPEAKING What animal is this? How would you describe it? What special characteristics does it have? Discuss with a partner.

2 SPEAKING Work in pairs. Look at the photos and discuss the questions.

1 What do you think has happened?
2 What are the people doing?
3 How do you think they are similar to a mole?

3 Read the article quickly. Name …

1 the year Los Topos began: ______
2 three countries where they have worked: ______
3 how many of Los Topos have died: ______

4 1.04 Read and listen to the article again and answer the questions.

1 Where did Los Topos begin?
2 When did Los Topos first work in the US?
3 What did they say about their work in Indonesia?
4 Why don't they go to every disaster?
5 What kind of training do Los Topos offer?

HUMAN MOLES

Moles are small animals that live underground and dig tunnels, looking for food. Sometimes humans also need to be like moles, but for a different reason – to save lives.

In 1985, there was a powerful earthquake in Mexico City. As often happens in earthquakes, many people were buried under fallen buildings and needed help. However, there weren't enough people to go and help them. So a group of young people decided to form a volunteer group. They started to dig into the rubble to try to find people and get them out. The group, who called themselves *Los Topos* ('the moles' in Spanish), quickly became well known for their bravery, and they started to travel to help at disaster zones in other places.

Since 1985 Los Topos have helped in places all around the world. At first they only worked in Mexico, but over the years they have been to Nepal, Haiti and the Philippines. In 2001, after the attack on the World Trade Center in New York, they came to the United States for the first time. And they went to Banda Aceh, Indonesia, in 2004, after the terrible tsunami that killed tens of thousands of people. They say that this was the most difficult work they have ever done. In 2017, they helped in Mexico City again, after another serious earthquake. Altogether, they have been to more than twenty countries.

The group has also grown – people in the group come and go, but on average it has about 40 members. It is very professional and includes doctors and other specialists, such as psychologists and engineers, but they are not paid for their work. They go to disaster areas when local governments and rescue groups cannot manage alone, and they also offer courses for people who want to become rescue workers. Los Topos members themselves pay most of what they need to travel to disaster zones – when they get there, they eat whatever they can and sleep wherever they can.

So far, not one member of Los Topos has lost their life – let's hope that this continues.

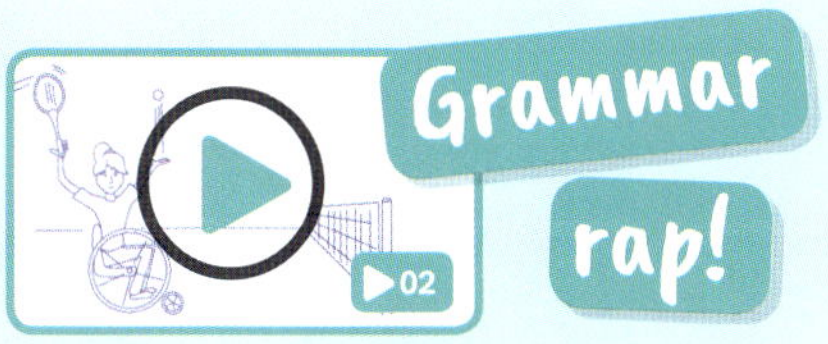

GRAMMAR
Present perfect vs. past simple

5 Look at the article on page 16 again. Which of the following events do we know happened at a specific point in time? Then complete the rules.

1 Los Topos formed?
2 Los Topos went to Nepal, Haiti and the Philippines?
3 Los Topos went to Banda Aceh?
4 Los Topos grew into a bigger organisation?

> **RULE:** When we talk about a specific point in time in the past, we use the [5] ____________________ .
> When we don't refer to a specific point in time, we often use the [6] ____________________ .

6 Complete the pairs of sentences. Use the past simple and the present perfect form of the verbs.

0 visit
- a I *have visited* Greece more than 20 times.
- b I first *visited* Greece in 1998.

1 win
- a He __________ already __________ three gold medals, and he hopes to win more.
- b He __________ a gold medal in the 2020 Olympics.

2 meet
- a My mum __________ a lot of interesting people.
- b My mum __________ Prince Harry ten years ago.

3 record
- a They __________ their last album two years ago.
- b They __________ more than 20 albums so far.

4 live
- a We __________ in Samoa when I was young.
- b We're living in Austria now, but we __________ in many different countries.

5 sign
- a She __________ just __________ a contract with a new e-publishing company.
- b She __________ the contract for her first book on her 21st birthday.

→ workbook page 11

VOCABULARY
Collocations

7 For each collocation, choose the two correct answers.

1 Which of these can you make?
a homework b a mistake c an appearance
2 Which of these things can you do?
a your best b a good time c work
3 Which of these things can you get?
a a bad day b a job c a reputation
4 Which of these things can you lose?
a a race b an idea c your life
5 Which of these can you take?
a a risk b a house c a photograph
6 Which of these can you form?
a a group b an opinion c a lesson

8 What verbs can go before the six words you didn't choose in Exercise 7? Think of at least one verb for each word.

9 SPEAKING Talk to other people in the class. Ask and answer questions and complete the table.

Have you ever ... ? What happened?

Who did you ask?

What was the risk?

What did you lose?

Find someone who has ...	Who?	Details
made a big mistake.		
done some chores at home this week.		
got a job.		
lost something important.		
taken a big risk.		
formed a group.		

→ workbook page 12

WRITING
Someone you admire

10 Write a short passage about someone you have admired for some time. Include:

- how long you have known (about) them.
- what you admire about them.

DEVELOPING SPEAKING

1 1.05 **Look at the photos. What do you think the connection is between them? Listen and read to check.**

Mike: You know our music teacher, Mr Grimes? He's leaving our school next month.

Emma: Are you sure? I haven't heard anything.

Mike: Yes, I'm sure. Steve said so. Mr Grimes told his class in yesterday's lesson.

Emma: That's a shame. He's a good teacher. His lessons are fun – jokes, games, smiles, that sort of thing.

Mike: I know. He's one of the best. But he's leaving, and that's that. Still, I was thinking – maybe we could do something to thank him. He's taught us such a lot. It would be nice to say thank you.

Emma: That's a good idea. What kind of thing?

Mike: Well, maybe a little concert? We could play or sing something for him.

Emma: No, I don't think so, Mike. A concert is too much. Let's face it, none of us are really good singers or musicians.

Mike: I know. But I want to do something.

Emma: Oh, you'll think of something. You always do!

Mike: Well, here's another idea. We could each make a recording – well, those who want to – and say something that we remember from his lessons. Then we could choose a bit of music …

Emma: … that he told us about! Yes! Mike, that's great. You've got to make it happen.

Mike: Well, I'll start by talking to the others, and find out what they think.

Emma: I'll help you if I can. You know what? I think everyone's going to love this, Mike. Really. Well done.

2 Read the dialogue again and answer the questions.

1. What is the news about Mr Grimes?
2. Why does Mike think it would be nice to say thank you to him?
3. What does Emma think of Mike's first idea?
4. What does Emma think of Mike's second idea?

3 SPEAKING **Discuss the questions in pairs.**

1. Is Mike right to want to say thank you to the teacher?
2. Do you think the recording is a better idea than the concert? Why or why not?

Phrases for fluency

4 Find the underlined expressions in the dialogue and use them to complete the conversations.

1. A That new girl, Sally – she likes you!
   B No, [1] ________________ .
   A [2] ________________ ? I have a feeling she likes you a lot.
   B No. She never smiles at me. And she criticises me a lot, doesn't laugh at my jokes, [3] ________________ .
2. A Oh, you got it wrong again!
   B I know. [4] ________________ , I'm no good at computer games.
   A [5] ________________ ? We just need a rest. Let's go and watch some TV.
   B OK, but I don't want to play this game again, OK? I'm useless at it, [6] ________________ !

FUNCTIONS
Offering encouragement

KEY LANGUAGE

That's a great idea. You've got to make it happen.
You should definitely do it. I'll help you if you want.

5 Complete the mini-dialogues using the sentences from the Key Language box.

1. **Jake** I'm not sure I can do this homework on my own.
   Paula ________________
2. **Carmen** Do you think Steve would like to have a party for his birthday?
   Adrian Yes, I do. ________________
3. **Millie** I've got an idea to get money for the school. I'd like to put on a play.
   Javier Oh, yes, brilliant! ________________
4. **Seb** You know I'm learning the guitar? Do you think I should enter the talent show?
   Harry Yes! ________________

6 In pairs, write a new short dialogue, using the sentences from the Key Language box. Choose one of these ideas or your own idea.

- a surprise party for your mum
- an outing with your friends
- a present for someone in hospital

7 SPEAKING **Act out your dialogue from Exercise 6.**

PRONUNCIATION
Intonation and sentence stress Go to page 120.

LIFE COMPETENCIES

Everywhere you go, there are people who are doing great things that improve other people's lives. Saying thank you is a simple way to show you recognise (and appreciate) these great things.

1 ▶ 03 Watch the video. What two small but important words does Anna talk about?

2 ▶ 03 Watch again and match the people with what they do.

1 ☐	Anna's mum	a	teaches Maths
2 ☐	Anna's dad	b	plays for free at parties
3 ☐	Mr Ward	c	listens well
4 ☐	Dave	d	makes breakfast in bed for Anna

3 Look at this poster. What does Quickshop supermarket want people to do?

Quickshop

LOCAL HEROES!

Everybody knows a community hero: the teen next door who spends her summers helping at the hospital; the neighbour who helps out at the local school every day; the friend who picks up litter in the town centre.

Quickshop has just celebrated its 100th birthday, and to celebrate we want to give a special award to the people who work quietly to make our lives better.

Local Heroes are everywhere – we just need your help to find them!

4 SPEAKING **Read these posts on the Quickshop website. Who do Julia and Milo think should win the award? Why? Discuss in pairs.**

SEARCH

Quickshop

About New Food Entertainment Stories

My uncle organises our football team. He does everything. We have football practice twice a week and he teaches us how to play better and to understand that winning isn't everything. He drives us to our matches, shouts encouragement and, after the game, takes our shirts home to wash them. – ***Julia***

Mrs Wilkins is the lollipop lady at the primary school. Every day, she helps the children cross the road because it's very dangerous. My mum says that Mrs Wilkins helped her cross the road when she was little, which was a long time ago! In the sun, wind and rain, Mrs Wilkins is always there, making sure everyone gets to school safely. – ***Milo***

Me and my world

5 **Think of somebody you know who should win a Local Hero award.**

- What do they do?
- Why do they do it?
- Is an award a good way to say thank you?
- Can you think of another way to say thank you?

6 SPEAKING **Tell the rest of your class about your Local Hero.**

TIPS FOR RECOGNISING OTHERS' GOOD WORK

- Make a list of all the places you go to. Think of someone special who helps to run this place.
- It's nice to explain how the person helped you – 'Because of you, I can …'.
- Sometimes simply saying thank you with a smile is enough.

2 A GOOD EDUCATION

OBJECTIVES

FUNCTIONS:
asking and giving / refusing permission to do something

GRAMMAR:
present perfect with *for* and *since*; *a*, *an*, *the* or no article

VOCABULARY:
school subjects; verbs about thinking

Get THINKING

Watch the video and think: how do you learn best?

1

2

3

4

READING

1 **Look at the photos. Does your school have these rooms or places?**

2 SPEAKING **Write a list of all the things you think a school should offer as well as a good education. Then compare with a partner.**

A school should offer students the chance to talk about any problems they might have in their lives.

3 **Look at the photos and the title on the next page. Why do you think this boy is the 'loneliest schoolboy in Britain'? Read the text quickly to check your ideas.**

4 2.01 **Read and listen to the article again. Choose the correct answer to these questions.**

1 What do we learn about the Out Skerries Islands from the text?
   A They are on the coast of Scotland.
   B There is a small airport.
   C It takes two and a half hours to get to the nearest town.
   D There is one shop on the island.

2 Why is Aron the only child at the school?
   A No other children live on the islands.
   B The government can't afford to send more children there.
   C The other children are taught by their parents.
   D The other children are too old for the school.

3 Why do some people complain about Aron's education?
   A They think it's not good for him to have no friends at the school.
   B They don't think he's learning the right things.
   C They think it costs too much.
   D They think he should be sent to private school.

4 How has the island changed over the last ten years?
   A There are more shops.
   B More families are coming to the island.
   C It's not as safe as it was.
   D There is less work there.

5 **Think of three questions you would like to ask Aron and write them in your notebook.**

What's the best part of your school day?
Do you miss your brothers?
Do you like always coming first in every test?

6 SPEAKING **Work in pairs. Take turns to be Aron. Ask and answer your questions from Exercise 5.**

What's the best part of your school day?

PE. I love being outside.

THE LONELIEST SCHOOLBOY IN BRITAIN

Imagine a school where you are the only student – where you come first in every test. Welcome to the life of ten-year-old Aron Anderson, who goes to school in Out Skerries, a group of small, remote islands in Scotland. Aron has been the only boy at his school for two months.

The Out Skerries Islands, which are around 280 km from the coast of Scotland, are home to about 70 people. The nearest town is Lerwick on the Shetland Islands. You can only get there by boat and it takes two and a half hours. Apart from Aron's school, there are two shops, a church and a community hall on the islands.

Aron isn't the only child on the islands and he hasn't always been the only student at the school. Until July there were several other children there, including Aron's two brothers. But now they are older, so they go to the secondary school in Lerwick. They only go back to their homes at the weekend. Aron has been the only student since September.

The school is very small. It has two classrooms, an art room, a music room and a library. Each week Aron studies Maths, English, Science and Art with the same teacher. She also gives him PE lessons. This is usually an hour-long walk around the islands. He also has the school playground all to himself. Of course, there is one problem. He has no one to play with.

What's more, Aron's education isn't cheap. It costs the UK government £75,357 each year. That is twice the price it costs parents to send a child to Britain's most famous private school, Eton. Some people want to close down the school. They think it is too much money to spend on one child's education.

Aron has lived in Out Skerries since he was born and loves the outdoor life. He enjoys exploring the islands on his bike and diving into the sea from the pier. Like most boys his age, he also likes watching TV and playing on his games console.

But his mother, who works in one of the shops on the islands, is worried that Aron might get lonely. She would like to see more families with children coming to live there. A lot of people have moved away since the local salmon factory closed ten years ago. That's why there are so few children on the islands and why Aron has found himself being known as the loneliest schoolboy in Britain.

THINK values

Learning for life

7 **Read the statements. Tick (✓) the things that you think Aron is probably not learning at his school.**

1 Everyone is different and that's a good thing. ☐
2 Teamwork is important to achieve things in life. ☐
3 We need to learn to respect the natural world. ☐
4 It is important to be friendly and help others. ☐
5 It is important to know how to spend time on your own. ☐
6 It's good to learn how to get on with people of different ages. ☐

8 SPEAKING **Compare your ideas with a partner.**

I think he is learning how to get on with people of different ages.
Why?
Well, he has all that time with just his teacher.
Yes, I agree with you.

9 SPEAKING **In small groups, discuss these questions.**

1 Which of the things from the list in Exercise 7 do you think are important to learn?
2 What would you add to your personal list of important things to learn?

GRAMMAR
Present perfect with *for* and *since*

1 **Look again at the article on page 21. Find all the sentences in the present perfect.**

2 **Complete the sentences below with *for* and *since*. Then complete the rules.**

1 Aron has lived in Out Skerries ______ he was born.

2 Aron has been the only boy at his school ______ two months.

> **RULE:** In the present perfect, we use:
> - [3]______ to talk about a period of time.
> - [4]______ to refer to the point in time when an action started.

3 **When do we use *for* and when do we use *since*? Complete the chart.**

~~a month~~ | ~~last summer~~ | a long time | an hour
a year | days | Friday | I phoned you | many years
2014 | yesterday | your birthday

for	*a month*	______	______
	______	______	______
since	*last summer*	______	______
	______	______	______

4 **Complete the sentences. Use the present perfect form of the verbs and *for* or *since*.**

1 I ____________ (be) at my new school ____________ last December.

2 Fatima ____________ (not see) Michael ____________ several weeks.

3 They ____________ (not write) us an email ____________ three months.

4 I ____________ (have) this camera ____________ I was ten.

5 **Write sentences using the present perfect with *for* or *since* and the words in brackets.**

1 They are at the youth club. (three hours)

2 Joanne and I are good friends. (primary school)

3 She plays in the volleyball team. (two months)

4 I ought to see a doctor. I'm sick. (a week)

5 I don't hear a lot from Silvia. (last October)

→ workbook page 18

VOCABULARY
School subjects

6 2.02 **Match the school subjects in the list with the photos. Write 1–12 in the boxes. Then listen and check.**

A

G

B

H

C

I

D

J

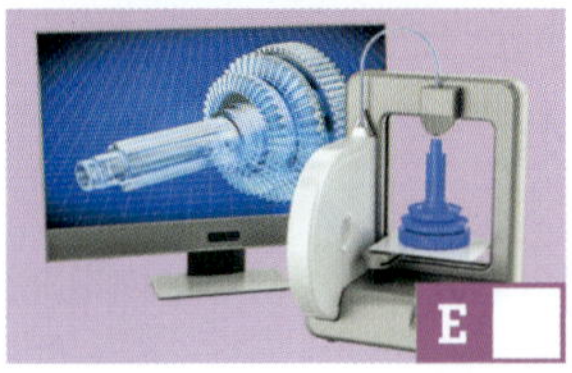
E

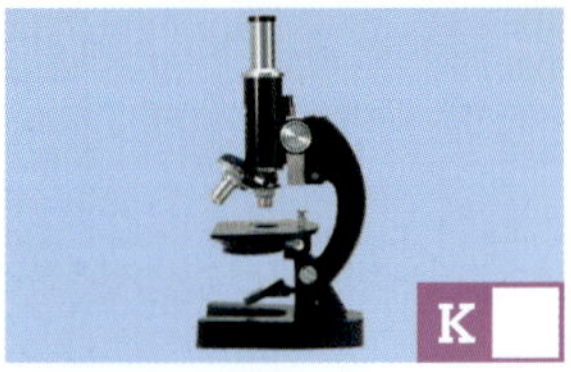
K

F

L

1 Science (Physics, Biology and Chemistry)
2 Music | 3 Art Education | 4 Drama
5 Design and Technology | 6 Geography
7 English | 8 PE (Physical Education)
9 ICT (Information and Communication Technology)
10 Maths | 11 History | 12 Spanish

7 SPEAKING **Answer the questions. Take notes. Then compare your answers with a partner.**

1 Which are your favourite subjects? Which don't you like? Why?

2 Which of the subjects are you studying this year?

3 How long have you studied each subject for?

→ workbook page 20

LISTENING

8 **Read the list of ten things to do this summer. Match four of the activities with the pictures.**

A

B

C

D

9 2.03 **Listen to Tom talking to his mother.**

1 Which things on the list does he want to do tomorrow?
2 What other things on the list does he mention?

TEN THINGS TO DO THIS SUMMER!

GET OFF YOUR PHONE AND GET OUTSIDE. THERE'S A WORLD OUT THERE. GO AND EXPLORE!

1 Climb a tree
2 Camp out in the wild
3 Run around in the rain
4 Eat an apple straight from a tree
5 Swing on a rope swing
6 Watch the sun rise
7 Climb a huge hill
8 Feed a bird from your hand
9 Swim in a river
10 Cook on a campfire

10 2.03 **Listen again. Mark the sentences T (true) or F (false).**

1 Tom's mum is surprised he wants her alarm clock. ____
2 Tom has less than two weeks to finish the challenge. ____
3 Tom found the list in a magazine. ____
4 Tom's mum thinks the challenge is a good idea. ____
5 Tom wants to climb the Malvern Hills with his friends. ____
6 Tom's mum isn't happy to take him to the Malvern Hills. ____

11 SPEAKING **Have you done any of the things on the list? Tell your partner.**

12 **Think of more things you could put on the list.**

FUNCTIONS

Asking and giving / refusing permission

13 **Put the dialogues in the correct order. Write the numbers 1–4.**

1 ☐ **Dad** Yes?
☐ **Dad** I'm afraid I need to use it, too.
☐ **Nick** Will you let me use your laptop?
☐ **Nick** Dad?

2 ☐ **Annie** Can I watch the football match tonight?
☐ **Annie** Can I ask you something, Mum?
☐ **Mum** Yes, of course you can.
☐ **Mum** Go ahead.

14 **Mark the sentences AP (asking permission), GP (giving permission) or RP (refusing permission).**

1 Will you let me use your mobile? ____
Yeah, sure. Of course I will. ____
2 Can I borrow your bike, please? ____
No, sorry. I need it. ____
3 Can I use your laptop, please? ____
Yes, you can, but I want it back tomorrow. ____
4 Is it OK if I borrow this necklace? ____
Yeah, but be really careful with it, OK? ____

ROLE PLAY **Work in pairs. Act out short conversations. Ask each other for permission. Use the ideas below, or come up with your own idea.**

borrow £20 | come with him/her
copy his/her homework
get some help with homework
use his/her tablet

READING

1 Look at the photos and answer the questions.

1 What do you think these people are thinking?
2 What would you say to them?

THE POWER OF 'YET'

1 Does life sometimes seem to be full of impossible problems? How many times, for example, do you find yourself saying things like 'I really don't understand this maths problem', or 'I can't get into the school team'?

Well, maybe it's time to introduce yourself to the power of 'yet'. By adding this simple word, you can change everything. 'I really don't understand this maths problem *yet*.' 'I can't get into the school team *yet*.'

Suddenly, the impossible becomes possible. You can imagine those things happening.

2 I read about a school that has changed the way it marks its students' exams. The school recognised that the old pass/fail system wasn't helping student motivation. If you passed, then great, but those students who didn't pass often felt like failures. So now students who don't get the score they need to pass don't see a big red F for fail on their exam papers; they see a 'Not yet' instead. That way the students feel that they are on a journey. They haven't reached the end, but they know that they are going the right way.

3 This kind of thinking is part of what experts call 'having a growth mindset'. People with a growth mindset don't concentrate on failure. They aren't worried by not getting things right the first time and are happy to keep trying until they do. They enjoy the challenge and believe they can change. In contrast, people who just focus on the failure have what the experts call 'a fixed mindset'. These people are always worried about failure and are happy to give up when things don't go right. They don't think that they are able to change. Clearly, it is better to have a growth mindset than a fixed mindset.

4 But don't worry if you think that you have a fixed mindset. You can train yourself to develop a growth mindset. Remember that it all starts with questioning the things you believe about yourself. Stop believing that you can't or you haven't and realise that you just can't or haven't *yet*. Once you start doing this, you'll wonder why you didn't do it before. It's one small but very powerful word.

2 2.04 **Read and listen to the text and answer the questions.**

1 How does the word yet make a difference?
2 Why did the school change the way it graded exams?
3 How do people with a growth mindset behave?
4 How are people with fixed mindsets different?
5 What's the first step needed to change from a fixed to a growth mindset?

3 SPEAKING **Make a list of three things you would like to be better at. Work with a partner and discuss how you could achieve these things.**

I'd like to be really good at the guitar.

Find time to practise for an hour every day.

Get lessons off the internet.

Learn to play your favourite songs.

Train to TH!NK

Learning about texts

4 Choose the best description of this text.

A an adventure story to entertain the reader
B an ad to sell the reader something
C a magazine article to give the reader information
D a letter to persuade the reader to do something

5 Choose the title that best sums up the content of each paragraph. Write 1–4. There is one extra title.

A ☐ A real-life example
B ☐ You can change
C ☐ The best advice is always free
D ☐ It's all about 'yet'
E ☐ Two ways of thinking

GRAMMAR
a, an, the or no article

6 **Look at the sentences from the magazine article. Underline *a, an, the* and the nouns that come after these articles. Then go through the sentences again and circle the nouns with no article. Finally, complete the rules with *a, an, the,* – (no article).**

Does life sometimes seem to be full of impossible problems?

I read about a school that has changed the way it marks its students' exams. The school recognised that the old pass/fail system wasn't helping.

The students feel that they are on a journey.

> **RULE:** We use [1]______ or [2]______ + a singular countable noun when the listener/reader doesn't know exactly which thing we are talking about.
> *You can have* ***an apple*** *or* ***a banana.***
> *We've got* ***a new car.***
> [3]______ + noun when it is clear which thing(s) or person/people we are talking about.
> ***The apples in this pie*** *are from our garden.*
> ***The bananas that I bought*** *yesterday are horrible.*
> [4]______ + plural countable noun or + uncountable noun, when we are talking about things in general.
> ***Bananas*** *are sweeter than* ***apples. Chocolate*** *isn't good for you.*

7 **Complete each sentence with *a, an, the* or – (no article).**

0 She is __*a*__ good student.
1 She eats a lot of ______ fruit and ______ vegetables.
2 ______ book that you gave me was really good.
3 I have ______ idea. Let's watch ______ new Beyoncé video.
4 I never drink ______ coffee – I hate it.
5 I like lots of sports, but ______ sport I like most is ______ tennis.

8 **Complete the text with *a, an, the* or –.**

[0]__–__ People need to drink. Of course [1]______ orange juice and [2]______ apple juice are very popular, but they are not always [3]______ good choice. [4]______ Orange juice has got a lot of sugar in it, so don't drink too much of it. The best drink for your brain is [5]______ water. [6]______ glass of water is the best drink you can get, but [7]______ water that you drink needs to be fresh and clean.

→ workbook page 19

VOCABULARY
Verbs about thinking

9 **Find these verbs in a dictionary and write their definitions in your notebook.**

believe | concentrate | guess
imagine | realise | recognise
remember | suppose | think | wonder

10 **Choose the correct words.**

1 The task was very difficult. I had to *remember / think* about it for a long time.
2 Come on, don't be silly. I don't *believe / realise* in ghosts!
3 Can you *imagine / concentrate* how great it must be to live at the beach?
4 When the teacher asked the question a different way, I *supposed / realised* that I knew the answer!
5 Did they really say they are moving to New York? I don't *suppose / believe* it!
6 I haven't seen her for six years. I don't think I would *realise / recognise* her.
7 I have no idea what the answer is. I'll just have to *recognise / guess.*
8 I was so tired that I found it hard to *think / concentrate* on the test.
9 Have you ever *wondered / believed* why I haven't phoned you for months?
10 If we want to get there faster, I *wonder / suppose* we should take a taxi.

PRONUNCIATION
Word stress Go to page 120.

11 SPEAKING **Work in pairs. Ask and answer the questions.**

1 Are there any places where you can think really well or not well at all?
2 Does music help you to concentrate or make it difficult for you to concentrate? Does it matter what kind of music it is?
3 In what situations can you imagine things really well? Do you find it difficult to use your imagination sometimes?
4 Do you find it difficult to remember things sometimes? What sort of things?
5 Have you ever tried meditation? Do you think meditating is useful?

→ workbook page 20

TH!NK

Schools with a difference

Culture

1 **Look at the photo and the title. What do you think is different about this school?**

2 2.07 **Read and listen to the article. Which school is the oldest? Which school is the newest?**

Schools with a difference

Every year Bangladesh is hit by heavy rains which cause large **floods** across the country. At these times life becomes difficult for millions of people who have no electricity or clean water. Many schools in these areas are forced to close. Shidhulai Swanirvar Sangstha is a **charity** which has provided education to more than 70,000 children with their **floating** schools since 2002. Each morning a school boat picks up children from nearby villages and when every child is on board, lessons can begin. In some of the lessons children learn about climate change and about protecting the environment. The charity has around 100 **solar**-powered boats and each one is fitted with a small library, a computer and internet access. The teachers also teach adults how to use the computers.

Each year more than 4,000 of India's poorest children get their education on the platforms of the country's railway stations. The idea for the Train Platform School came from a teacher called Inderjit Khurana. She wanted to do something for the children she met **begging** on the train she took to work each morning. She knew that without education, these children had no hope for their futures, and in 1985, she set up the first school and the school still exists today. Music and drama are among the **methods** used to teach the children how to read and write. When the children are ready, they can transfer to a full-time school. The schools also provide the children with food and medicine when it is needed.

You won't find any books at the West Philadelphia School of the Future in the US. Instead, all students have their own computers and learn on specially designed apps. Teachers don't use **traditional** whiteboards – they use hi-tech Smart Boards. When the school opened in 2006, both the teachers and the students found it difficult. They didn't know how to use all the technology. Since then the school has **improved** and these days students get high marks in Maths and reading, making it a very popular school with parents. The people who started the school hope that other schools will follow their example.

3 SPEAKING **What makes your school different? Discuss in pairs. What could you change to make your school more unique?**

4 Read the article again. Complete the sentences with *Bangladesh, India* or *US*.

1 The children here learn at stations. ______
2 This school uses the most modern technology. ______
3 The weather makes life difficult here sometimes. ______
4 This school uses solar power. ______
5 It's difficult to get a place at this school. ______
6 This school wants other schools to be like them. ______
7 Children here have 'floating' lessons. ______
8 The children get more than just an education. ______

5 VOCABULARY There are eight highlighted words in the article. Match the words with these meanings. Write the words.

1 of or from the sun ______
2 got better ______
3 usual, things as they have always been ______
4 when there is too much water on the land ______
5 staying above water ______
6 ways of doing something ______
7 asking people for money in the streets ______
8 an organisation which helps people, animals, the environment etc. ______

WRITING

An email describing your school routine

1 INPUT Read Ruby's email. Then answer the questions.

1 How does Ruby feel about her new class?
2 What does Ruby think of Nathan and why?
3 How does her work for school compare to last year?
4 What subject does she get a lot of homework for, and how does she feel about it?
5 Does Ruby think you've got less schoolwork than her?

Ruby
ruby@yourmail.com

Hi!

Hi there!

I hope this finds you well. I haven't heard from you since the beginning of the holidays. Are you enjoying your new school?

I am, big time! I'm in a class with all my friends again – Rosa, Liz, Jacob and all the others. There's a new kid in my class, too. His name's Nathan and he's from Nantes in France. His mother is working in the UK for two years, and the whole family have come over. He's cool. We have lots of fun together.

But of course, it's not all fun. We've got important exams this year so there's a lot of work to do. I'm spending more time at school than last year, and I come home at 5.45 three times a week. We're also getting a lot more homework, especially for Art. But I love the projects we do in this class!

Well, I guess it's not so different for you. If you've got a bit of time, please let me know how things are going. I'd really like to know what life at school is like for you. And remember, please, you've got a friend in Brighton who would really like to get mail from you more often!

Write soon!

Ruby

2 Find sentences in the email where Ruby writes about these things. What tense does she use in those sentences? Why does she use it?

a asks how you feel about your new school
b talks about Nathan's mother
c compares school this year to last year
d talks about the amount of homework this year

3 Put the words in the right order. Write the sentences. What tense are they in and why?

1 new / too / class / kid / There's / a / my / in
______
2 a week / at / three times / come home / 5.45 / I
______
3 love / projects / I / class / But / the / do / this / in / we
______

4 ANALYSE Match the four paragraphs of Ruby's email with the content.

Paragraph 1	a Ruby's new class
Paragraph 2	b a request to write soon
Paragraph 3	c an introduction
Paragraph 4	d work this year compared to last

5 PLAN Read Ruby's email again. Make notes with your own ideas on how:

a to answer the question in her introduction
b to describe your new class (new school? classmates?)
c to compare your work this year to last year's
d to say how you feel about your subjects (any subjects you particularly like/don't like? Why?)
e you could finish your email (what do you want to know from Ruby?)

6 PRODUCE Write an email to Ruby (about 200 words). Look at your notes from Exercise 5 and make sure you include all your ideas. Make sure you use the present simple when necessary.

B1 Preliminary for Schools

READING

Part 6: Open cloze

→ workbook page 115

1 **For each question, write the correct answer. Write one word for each gap.**

The Tan-y-Bryn *Outdoor Adventure Centre*

The Tan-y-Bryn Outdoor Adventure Centre is on the island of Anglesey in North Wales. [1]______ opening its doors in 1975, it has welcomed thousands of young people from all over the UK to enjoy fun, education and adventure in the beautiful Welsh countryside. Whether they are climbing up Mount Snowdon, swimming in the Menai Straits [2]______ birdwatching in the woodlands, visitors enjoy hands-on experiences they [3]______ never forget.

For school groups, youth clubs and families the Centre offers comfortable accommodation for [4]______ to 50 children and 10 adults. It also provides a full breakfast, lunch and dinner to make [5]______ no one goes hungry. Safety is a top priority – there [6]______ never been a serious accident at the Centre.

LISTENING

→ workbook page 17

Part 1: 3-option multiple choice

2 2.08 **For each question, choose the correct answer.**

1 What did Sally buy at the shops?

2 What time is it?

3 How did Brian get to work?

4 Which lesson did Fred enjoy most?

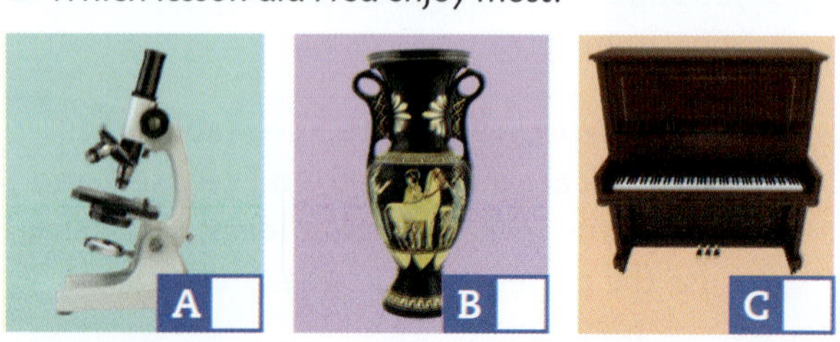

5 What month is Tom's brother's birthday?

6 What's the score in the football match?

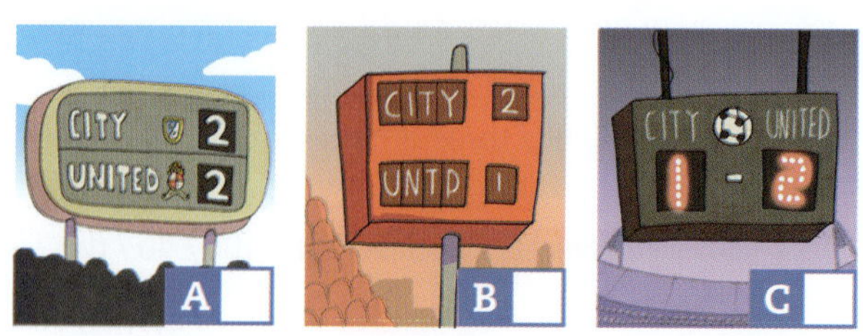

7 Which man are the police looking for?

TEST YOURSELF UNITS 1 & 2

VOCABULARY

1 Complete the sentences with the words in the list. There are two extra words.

active | believe | brave | creative | formed | got | guess | lost | realise | recognise | take | wonder

1 I think I ______________________ the wrong opinion of her. She's actually really nice.
2 My grandmother's quite old, but she's still very ______________________ – she's always doing things!
3 He ______________________ the race by less than one second.
4 I didn't like the birthday cards in the shop, so I decided to be ______________________ and make one.
5 It's strange that Eve isn't here. I ______________________ where she is.
6 It's midday! Wow! I didn't ______________________ it was so late.
7 I didn't know the answer, so I had to ______________________ .
8 She didn't run away when the tiger was running towards her – she was very ______________________ .
9 I'm sure he saw me, but he didn't say hello. Maybe he didn't ______________________ me.
10 I've ______________________ a reputation for always being late. I don't think it's fair.

/10

GRAMMAR

2 Complete the sentences with the words in the list. You need to write the correct form of the verbs.

bus | the bus | not open (x2) | not see (x2)

1 My best friend gave me my present this morning, but I ______________________ it yet.
2 I'm tired – I don't want to walk. Let's go by ______________________ .
3 She was at school today? Really? I ______________________ her there.
4 There was a sign on the gate that said 'No entry!', so I ______________________ it.
5 There's a new film on Netflix, but I ______________________ it yet.
6 We were late because ______________________ arrived 45 minutes late.

3 Find and correct the mistake in each sentence.

1 Can I have a glass of an orange juice, please?
2 I've travelled to already more than twenty capital cities.
3 We've lived here since ten months.
4 I've gone to the cinema last night.
5 This is my computer. I had it for two years.
6 It's important to drink a lot of the water if you want to be healthy.

/12

FUNCTIONAL LANGUAGE

4 Complete the mini-dialogues with the words in the list.

afraid | Can | definitely | go | idea | Let's | OK | thinking

1 A ______________________ I use your pen, please?
B Sorry, I'm ______________________ I'm using it right now.
2 A ______________________ go and see the new Marvel film tonight.
B That's a great ______________________ !
3 A I'm ______________________ about doing a walk for charity. What do you think?
B Yes, you should ______________________ do it.
4 A Is it ______________________ if I use your dictionary?
B Yes, of course, ______________________ ahead.

/8

MY SCORE /30

22–30 😊 | 10–21 😐 | 0–9 😣

3 ON THE SCREEN

OBJECTIVES

FUNCTIONS: comparing things and actions; asking for and offering help

GRAMMAR: comparative and superlative adjectives (review); (*not*) *as … as*; making a comparison stronger or weaker; adverbs

VOCABULARY: types of films; types of TV programmes; expressions with *get*

Get THINKING

Watch the video and think: what's your favourite form of entertainment?

READING

1 **Match the words in the list with the photos. Write 1–6 in the boxes.**

1 concert | **2** cinema | **3** play | **4** sports event
5 TV programme | **6** video game

2 SPEAKING **Which of these kinds of entertainment do you like? Tell your partner.**

3 SPEAKING **Work in small groups. Talk about the things in Exercise 1. Say why people like or don't like them. Use the words in the list to help you.**

crowds | enjoyable | expensive
friends | fun | interesting | relaxing

I think people enjoy going to the cinema because it is relaxing.

4 **Look at the pictures and the title of the article on the next page. What do you think the article is about?**

A a director
B an actor
C a type of film

5 3.01 **Read and listen to the article and check your ideas.**

6 **Read the article again. Find:**

1 two examples of things that influenced Tim Burton
2 the reason people were upset when Burton chose Michael Keaton for *Batman*
3 two examples of types of film that Burton has made
4 an example of creative work that Burton does apart from directing films

A new kind of SUPERHERO

Tim Burton is one of the most famous American film directors. His most popular films include: *Batman* (1989), *Edward Scissorhands* (1990), *Batman Returns* (1992) and *Dumbo* (2019). In 1990, he got a Daytime Emmy Award for his cartoon series *Beetlejuice* and in 1991 he got a Hugo Award for *Edward Scissorhands*.

Tim grew up watching horror films and cartoons. He read Edgar Allan Poe's horror stories and he loved drawing. He also made short films in his back garden. After leaving school, Burton studied animation. Then, he got a job at Walt Disney studios. He was a very good animator, but he didn't draw in the Disney style. So he left Disney and started to make his own films.

One of his most successful films is *Batman*. At first, people were upset when Tim Burton chose the comedy actor Michael Keaton to play Batman. Batman is a superhero who is taller and stronger than ordinary men, and Michael Keaton was too short. At 1.75 m, he was in fact the shortest actor ever to play Batman. However, the film was very successful and everybody loved Michael Keaton as Batman.

One of Tim Burton's most interesting characters is Edward Scissorhands. The idea for the character came from a drawing that Burton made in high school. Edward isn't human and he has got scissors instead of hands. In the film, Johnny Depp plays Edward. However, his character in the film is not as scary as Tim Burton's original drawing.

In one of his latest films, *Dumbo*, Dumbo the elephant has got bigger ears than the other elephants and they laugh at him. However, his big ears are an advantage. He can fly. This new film is more exciting than the old Disney film, but the CGI elephant is not as cute as the cartoon elephant in the 1941 film. There are some changes in the plot, but the new film is still as sad as the old one.

Tim Burton has directed many other films, including some of the best-loved children's stories like *Charlie and the Chocolate Factory* and *Alice in Wonderland*. He still produces films today, and sometimes he shows some of his drawings and cartoons at exhibitions around the world.

THINK values

Preconceived ideas

7 **Read the sentences. How much do you agree with each one? Write a number: 1 (I agree), 2 (I'm not sure) or 3 (I don't agree).**

1. If there is a film about a real-life famous person, the actor should look as much like that person as possible. ☐
2. I won't go to see a new film if there is an actor in it that I don't like. ☐
3. Cheap things are never worth buying. ☐
4. There are some shops where I would never buy clothes. ☐
5. It's crazy not to like someone because of the way they speak. ☐

8 SPEAKING **Work in groups. Compare your ideas.**

I don't agree with number 1. It's impossible to find actors who look the same.

Do you think so? I agree with it. I think they should wear make-up to make them look very similar.

GRAMMAR

Comparative and superlative adjectives (review)

1 Complete these sentences from the article on page 31 with the correct form of the words in the list.

big | exciting | short | strong | tall

1 Batman is a superhero who is ______________ and ______________ than ordinary men.
2 At 1.75 m, he was in fact ______________ actor to ever play Batman.
3 Dumbo the elephant has got ______________ ears than the other elephants.
4 This new film is ______________ the old Disney film.

(*not*) *as* ... *as* comparatives

2 Look at the examples of (*not*) *as* ... *as* to compare things. Answer the questions. Then complete the rule.

His character in the film is not as scary as Tim Burton's original drawing.
The new film is still as sad as the old one.

1 Which is scarier: the original drawing or the character in the film?
2 Is the new film sadder than the old film?

RULE: When we want to say that two things are (not) the same, we can use (*not*) [3]______ + adjective + [4]______ .

3 Complete each sentence with your own ideas.

1 a Football isn't as exciting as *skiing* .
b Football is more exciting than *golf* .
2 a English is easier than ______________ .
b English isn't as easy as ______________ .
3 a Watching TV isn't as good as ______________ .
b Watching TV is better than ______________ .

4 Complete the second sentence so it has the same meaning as the first. Use the word in brackets.

0 Ben's sister is younger than him. (old)
Ben's sister *isn't as old as* him.
1 Travelling by train is faster than travelling by bus. (slow)
Travelling by train ______________ travelling by bus.
2 Tom is 1.65 m. Sue is 1.65 m, too. (tall)
Tom ______________ Sue.
3 Dogs are noisier than cats. (quiet)
Dogs ______________ cats.
4 This mobile phone costs €225. And the bicycle costs €225, too. (expensive)
The mobile phone ______________ the bicycle.
5 Jo thinks Geography is easier than History. (difficult)
Jo thinks Geography ______________ History.
6 My room is tidier than yours. (untidy)
My room ______________ yours.

PRONUNCIATION
Words ending in /ə/ Go to page 120.

→ workbook page 28

VOCABULARY

Types of films

5 Write the types of films in the list under the pictures.

action film | animated film | comedy | documentary | horror film
romantic comedy (rom com) | science fiction (sci-fi) | thriller

1 ______________

2 ______________

3 ______________

4 ______________

5 ______________

6 ______________

7 ______________

8 ______________

6 SPEAKING Can you think of an example of each type of film? Are any of your examples more than one type?

Spies in Disguise is an action film.

→ workbook page 30

LISTENING

7 🔊 3.04 **Listen to Part 1 of an interview. Why is Emma Harding a guest on the radio show?**

8 🔊 3.05 **Listen to Part 2 of the interview. For each question, choose the correct answer.**

1 Emma says that making a Lego film
 A takes a lot of time.
 B is far easier than you think.
 C requires lots of drawing.

2 When she was making the film, Emma
 A used her own camera.
 B didn't have any lights.
 C had some help from a friend.

3 Emma says that her film is
 A 10 seconds long.
 B 18 seconds long.
 C 20 seconds long.

GRAMMAR

Making a comparison stronger or weaker

9 Read the sentences. Choose the phrase that has a different meaning from the other two. Then complete the rule.

0 Eighteen photos look *a lot* / *much* / *(a little)* better than ten photos.
1 Together we made the script *a little* / *a lot* / *a bit* better.
2 I'm sure it's *a little* / *much* / *far* more difficult than it looks.

> **RULE:** Use [3]______ / [4]______ / ***far*** to make a comparative stronger.
> Use ***a bit*** / [5]______ to make a comparative weaker.

10 Rewrite these sentences using the words in brackets.

1 Sharks are more dangerous than dolphins. (a lot)
2 My brother is taller than me. (a bit)
3 My new phone's better than my old one. (far)
4 Her hair is longer than yours. (a little)
5 The film's more exciting than the book. (much)

11 Write sentences comparing these things. Use *much* / *far* / *a lot* or *a bit* / *a little*.

0 watching TV / reading a book (interesting / easy)
 I think watching TV is a lot more interesting than reading a book – and it's far easier, too.
1 gorillas / snakes (dangerous / beautiful)
2 English / Art (difficult / interesting)
3 my country / US (big / beautiful)

→ workbook page 29

WordWise: Expressions with *get*

12 Look at the sentences from the unit so far. Choose the correct meaning of *get* in each one.

1 Then you need to get yourself a camera.
2 He got a Daytime Emmy Award for his cartoon series *Beetlejuice*.
3 I couldn't wait to get home and tell my mum.
4 I still get emotional now when I think about it.

a become
b received
c arrive
d obtain, buy

13 Use a phrase from the list to complete each sentence.

> get a drink | get angry | get home
> got better | got bored | got there

1 The film was terrible – after 20 minutes, I ______ and fell asleep.
2 I was really late for school – when I ______ , it was already ten o'clock!
3 There's still a long way to go. I don't think we'll ______ before midnight.
4 He was ill for about a week, but then he ______ , I'm happy to say.
5 It was just a joke. Please don't ______ with me!
6 If you want, we can ______ in that café in the town centre.

14 Match the questions and answers.

1 Let's go and get a drink. ☐
2 When do you get angry with people? ☐
3 Do you ever get bored watching TV? ☐
4 What time do you get to school? ☐
5 Do you ever get a cold? ☐

a When they say things I don't like.
b Usually about eight o'clock.
c OK. The shop over there sells water.
d Sometimes – in winter, usually.
e Only when it's a programme I don't like.

→ workbook page 30

READING

1 Read the article quickly. Write the titles in the correct spaces 1–4.

A The rise in screen time
B TV as a family activity
C The changing world of TV
D Non-stop drama

THE HISTORY OF watching TV

1 ______________

Television (TV) has been in people's homes since the 1930s, but our way of watching TV has changed significantly over the years. In the 1950s, families that had TVs, only had one TV set and three channels to choose from. Nowadays, we can watch a TV show on many different devices, anywhere and at any time of the day or night. Consequently, our generation is watching TV more frequently than any other generation before.

2 ______________

TVs were luxury items in the 1950s, and the families that did have one had to sit very close to it as the screens were very small.
Then in the 1960s, TVs became cheaper and more families owned one. Most people had a TV in their living room and families sat together and watched their favourite shows. Oh, and there was no 'Watch next episode' button. People had to wait patiently for a week to watch the next part of their favourite soap opera.

3 ______________

Then, in the mid-2000s, TV broadcasters started to make programmes available via the internet. It was called on-demand TV and became very popular because people could choose when they wanted to watch a programme. Now, you could watch an episode of a sitcom straight away. Instead of watching one episode, people happily binge-watched six hours of their favourite TV series in one afternoon. Drama series became like one long film. And if you missed a documentary or an episode of your favourite reality show, you could easily watch it online later.
During this decade, far fewer people sat down with their families to watch a TV show. However, people still preferred to watch major sports events (such as the FIFA World Cup) live.

4 ______________

In the 2010s, children and young adults began to watch much less broadcast TV than in the past. They watched their entertainment on smartphones, games consoles and via streaming services. This meant they could watch a show more easily at any time. Now, people spend more hours watching TV. In fact, the average person in Britain spends almost ten years of their life watching TV! As well as watching a show, they also need to read all the posts about it quickly, and tweet about it, too. This adds up to a lot more screen time.

2 3.06 **Read and listen to the text again. Answer the questions.**

1 Why did you sometimes have to wait seven days in the early years of TV to watch a programme?
2 How did 'on-demand' TV change the way people watch TV?
3 In the 2000s, which type of programme did people prefer to watch at the time it was broadcast?
4 What effect do social media have on the amount of time people spend looking at screens?

3 SPEAKING **Which statements are true for you? In groups, compare your ideas.**

1 I prefer to watch TV alone rather than with other people.
2 I sometimes binge-watch drama series.
3 I sometimes use social media to discuss TV programmes with friends.
4 I spend more time on a tablet or computer than I do in front of a TV.

GRAMMAR

Adverbs and comparative adverbs

4 Look at the sentences from the article. Complete them with the words in the list.

cheaper | easily | long | patiently

1 TVs became ______ .
2 People had to wait ______ for a week to watch the next episode.
3 Drama series became like one ______ film.
4 You could ______ watch it online later.

5 **Look again at the text on page 34 and find the adverbs. Then complete the rules with *adjective* and *adverb*.**

> **RULE:** Use an [1]______ to talk about a noun:
> *He's a slow runner.*
> Use an [2]______ to talk about a verb:
> *He runs slowly.*
> We usually form an [3]______ by adding *-ly* (or *-ily*) to the [4]______, but some adverbs are irregular: *fast* ➜ *fast*, *good* ➜ *well*.

6 **Write the adverbs.**

0 quick *quickly*
1 careful ______
2 clever ______
3 happy ______
4 good ______
5 bad ______
6 easy ______
7 fast ______

7 **Look at the examples of comparative adverbs from the text on page 34. Then complete the rules.**

1 This meant they could watch a show **more easily** at any time.
2 Our generation is watching TV **more frequently** than any other generation before.

> **RULE:** To form the comparative of most regular adverbs, add the word [3]______ before the adverb: *easily* ➜ *more easily*.
> If an adverb has one syllable, make the comparative by adding *-er*: *soon* ➜ *sooner*, *hard* ➜ *harder*, *fast* ➜ *faster*.
> - There are some irregular comparative adverbs: *badly* ➜ *worse*, *well* ➜ *better*.
> - Notice that the comparative of *early* is *earlier*.

8 **Complete the sentences. Use the comparative adverb forms of the words in brackets.**

0 Sue runs (fast) than me. *faster*
1 George writes ______ (clear) than me.
2 You need to do your homework ______ (careful) if you want to get good marks.
3 Sorry, I don't understand. Can you speak ______ (slow), please?
4 The party starts at ten o'clock, but you can come ______ (early) if you want to.
5 I only got 22% in the test, but you did even ______ (bad) than me!
6 Isabella always works ______ (hard) than the other kids.
7 Martina speaks English ______ (good) than I do.

➜ workbook page 29

VOCABULARY
Types of TV programmes

9 **Look at the different types of TV programmes. Can you think of an example for each one?**

cartoon

reality show

chat show

sitcom

drama series

soap (opera)

game show

sports programme

news

talent show

10 SPEAKING **Work in pairs. Ask and answer the questions.**

1 What kind(s) of programmes do you really like?
2 What kind(s) of programmes do you really NOT like?
3 What's your favourite programme at the moment? Why?
4 What's your least favourite programme at the moment? Why?
5 How do you watch TV programmes – on TV, on your phone, on a tablet …?

➜ workbook page 30

WRITING
A paragraph about your TV habits

11 **Write a paragraph about your TV habits.**

- Use your answers to the questions in Exercise 10 to help you.
- Try to use grammar and vocabulary from the unit (comparative adjectives, words for TV programmes, etc.).

DEVELOPING SPEAKING

1 🔊 3.07 **Look at the photo. Why do you think the girl is tired? Listen and read to check.**

Megan: Hi, Josh. Have you got a moment? I'd like some help with a Maths question.

Josh: Hey, Megan. Sure. How can I help? Is everything OK? Looks like you haven't slept for about a week!

Megan: Well, I didn't sleep much last night. Or the night before. In fact, I haven't slept well for three nights.

Josh: Why not?

Megan: It's that new drama – *The Big Show*. It came out last week. It's fantastic. And last night I watched it until ... well, quite late.

Josh: How late?

Megan: Well, three o'clock in the morning. I watched all 20 episodes in three nights.

Josh: Wow! I'm not surprised you're tired and can't concentrate.

Megan: But it's so good! Last night there were only two more episodes to watch, I had to keep going. It's like running a long race – it starts to hurt but you have to carry on! My parents always tell me not to give up halfway through something.

Josh: But you shouldn't stay up all night.

Megan: I know. But it's brilliant. Anyway – could you help me with the Maths problem? Please?

Josh: Here, have a look at this.

Megan: A book!?

Josh: Yes, it explains everything. Just don't fall asleep while you're reading it, OK?

Megan: Oh come on, Josh! Please help me.

Josh: Sorry, I can't. I've got to go now. So, you'll have to do it yourself after all. Oh, and guess what? You've got ten minutes to do it before the lesson starts!

2 Read the dialogue again and answer the questions.

1 What does Megan want Josh's help with?
2 What has Megan done for the last three nights?
3 What does she compare watching the TV series to?
4 What does Josh tell her to do to understand the Maths problem?

3 SPEAKING **Discuss the questions in pairs.**

1 Is it OK for Megan to ask Josh to help her?
2 Is her comparison with running a good one?
3 Was Josh right not to help Megan?

Phrases for fluency

4 Find the underlined expressions in the dialogue and use them to complete the conversation.

Jim Hi guys. [1]_________ ? I'm in the football team!
Mike You're joking!
Jim No, I'm not. [2]_________ . It's the team list.
Mike But you're not a good player, Jim. [3]_________ , you're terrible!
Alice Oh, [4]_________ , Mike! He's not so bad.
Susie That's right. And the school has picked him to play, so [5]_________ you're wrong, Mike.
Mike Well, I guess so.
Jim Yes. I'm good enough for the school team [6]_________ !

FUNCTIONS
Asking for and offering help

KEY LANGUAGE

Could you ... ?	Can you ... ?
Can I ... ?	Is everything OK / all right?

5 Look at these sentences. Are they asking for or offering help? Write A (asking) or O (offering).

1 Can you lend me a hand? ___
2 Can I help you at all? ___
3 Is everything OK? ___
4 Have you got a few minutes? ___

6 Complete the mini-dialogues using the expressions from the Key Language box.

1 **Maisie** _______ help me with my homework please, Mum?
Mum Of course, Maisie, what subject is it?
2 **Pablo** _______ give me a hand, Mr Terrence?
Mr Terrence No problem. _______
3 **Sofia** ______ have some ice cream, Grandma?
Grandma No, Sofia, dinner is almost ready.

7 SPEAKING **Work in pairs. Use the questions in the Key Language box and in Exercise 5 to act out conversations in a shop, at home, at school and in other places.**

LIFE COMPETENCIES

Everybody has got something they find really difficult. But just because it's hard doesn't mean we can't do it – whether it's getting better grades at school, improving at sport or even learning a new language. Commitment and determination can help us achieve our goals, no matter how large or small.

1 ▶ 09 Watch the video. How far did Kieran get in the 10 km race?

2 ▶ 09 Watch again and complete Kieran's notes.

Step 1: Identify goal

Step 2: Best thing about achieving my goal

Step 3: What may stop me

Step 4: How to make sure those things DON'T stop me

3 SPEAKING Work with a partner. What do you think of this advice? Are there any ideas you don't think are good?

How to achieve your goals:

1 Divide your main goal into smaller goals.
2 Make a weekly plan of action for each small goal.
3 Take the first step!
4 Expect some problems and be ready to solve them.
5 Ask friends and family for encouragement.
6 Review how well you're doing and make changes to your plan if necessary.
7 Stay focused!
8 Reward yourself!

4 Alex is shy, so people often think she's unfriendly. As a result, she doesn't have many friends. She'd like to make more friends, so she's going to follow the advice in Exercise 3. Complete her notes with your own ideas. Compare with a partner.

1 ______________________
2 ______________________
3 Start on Monday 12th.
4 ______________________
5 Tell Mum and my friend Katy about the plan. Update them every week.
6 Review the plan with Mum or Katy every Sunday.
7 Set calendar on mobile to remind me of plan every day.
8 ______________________

Me and my world

5 Choose one of the ideas from the list below that you would like to work on (or choose one of your own). Make notes like Alex's about how you're going to achieve your goal.

- Spend less time looking at screens
- Help more around the house
- Read more
- Eat more healthily

6 SPEAKING Tell your friends about your plans. Listen to each other and give ideas and advice.

TIPS FOR ACHIEVING YOUR GOALS

- Make a plan. It is a good way to ensure you have a clear idea of what you want to achieve.
- Be realistic when setting goals. Changing how you behave takes time.
- Reward yourself when you achieve something, but don't feel too bad and punish yourself if you don't.

4 ONLINE LIFE

Get THINKING

Watch the video and think:
do you post too many things on social media?

OBJECTIVES

FUNCTIONS: giving advice

GRAMMAR: indefinite pronouns (*everyone, no one, someone, etc.*); *all / some / none / any of them; should(n't), had better, ought to*

VOCABULARY: IT terms; language for giving advice

READING

1 SPEAKING **Work in pairs. Answer the questions.**

1 Which of these social networks do you know?
2 What do you think of them?
3 Do you know any other social networks?

2 SPEAKING **Read these statements about using social networks. Which of them are true for you? Discuss them with a partner.**

1 I've got a Facebook account but hardly ever use it.
2 I don't post many comments, but I like to read other people's posts.
3 I constantly check for updates on social media.
4 I sometimes post comments that I regret later.

3 **Look at the photos on the next page. What do you think the article is about? Read the article quickly to check your ideas.**

4 4.01 **Read and listen to the article about online behaviour again. Mark the statements T (true) or F (false).**

1 A digital footprint is like a footprint in sand because it disappears after time. ______
2 People who use the internet create an online history for themselves. ______
3 What you do online can lead to you receiving certain kinds of advertisements. ______
4 What you write online can be misunderstood by other people. ______
5 People should be careful about what personal information they include when they write online. ______
6 You can make life more difficult for thieves by not putting personal information online. ______
7 It's OK to put a credit card number in an email, but not a password. ______
8 It's possible not to leave a digital footprint if you go online. ______

5 SPEAKING **Work in pairs. Correct the false statements in Exercise 4.**

LEAVING FOOTPRINTS

Imagine you are walking in the sand on a beach somewhere, or through deep snow on a mountain. As you walk, you leave footprints where you've been. Later, of course, the footprints disappear. But imagine if they didn't – if your footprints stayed there forever. And imagine, too, that you left footprints everywhere you walked, including in your home and in your town – so that someone could see everywhere you've been. How happy would you be about that?

Well, that's what happens when you use technology – computers, mobile phones, tablets. It's your digital footprint – a record of where you've been and what you've seen that you leave when you go online. Your comments on social media, your retweets, the apps you use, the emails you send, everything you've searched for – all of them are part of your digital footprint, and other people can see your footprint, or it can be tracked in a database.

Does this matter? Why would anyone be interested in what you write on Twitter or post on Instagram? Well, companies who sell things are interested, that's for sure – they want to send you adverts for things they want you to buy. But apart from businesses, there are other reasons why your digital footprint should matter to you.

1 HOW PEOPLE SEE YOU

Of course, you have nothing to hide, but if people get information about you, they might pick bits to make you look good – or bad. Perhaps one day you write something silly online. Maybe you make a bad joke. Years later, it's found by the university you're applying to, and they don't think it's funny. Then what? Maybe they decide you're not the 'right' kind of person for them.

2 YOUR PRIVATE INFORMATION

Everyone has information about themselves that they don't want everyone to know (for example, you might share your school reports with your parents but not friends), but the internet doesn't make the same decisions that you would.

3 KEEPING YOUR MONEY SAFE

There are plenty of people looking at information about you, and some of them want to steal from you, but the less information you put out, the harder it is for them. Bank details, card numbers, passwords or PINs – none of them should be written in emails, text messages or anything else.

Overall, the message is: remember that you have a digital footprint, and think carefully before you click 'send' or 'post'. No one can go online and not leave a footprint – but with care, you can control it.

TH!NK values

Responsible online behaviour

6 **Read the statements. Write them in two lists under *Do* and *Don't*.**

1 Say bad things about other people online.
2 Talk to your teacher or another adult if you get bullied on social media.
3 Think carefully before you write a post about yourself or other people.
4 Write a post about someone when you are angry with them.
5 Write posts containing personal information about your family.
6 Think before you post a photo of yourself or someone else.

7 SPEAKING **Work in pairs. Compare your lists. Think of at least two more statements for each list.**

GRAMMAR
Indefinite pronouns (*everyone, no one, someone,* etc.)

1 Complete these sentences from the article on page 39. Find other examples of indefinite pronouns in the article.

1 Imagine, too, that you left footprints ______ you walked.
2 Perhaps one day you write ______ silly online.
3 ______ can go online and not leave a footprint.

2 Complete the table. Use the article on page 39 to help you. Then complete the rules with *some / any / no / every*.

everything	[1] ________	nothing	anything
everyone	someone	no one	[3] ________
everywhere	somewhere	[2] ________	anywhere

RULE: The words beginning with
- [4] ______ mean 'all' (people / things / places).
- [5] ______ mean that we don't know exactly which (person / thing / place).
- [6] ______ mean that we don't care or it doesn't matter which (person / thing / place).
- [7] ______ mean 'not any' (person / thing / place).

3 Complete the sentences with words from the table in Exercise 2.

1 Where's my pen? I've looked ____________, but I can't find it.
2 Using social media can be a real problem. ____________ should know that.
3 The teacher asked a question, but ____________ knew the answer.
4 ____________ has left a message for you at reception.
5 Ouch! There's ____________ in my eye!
6 I've no idea where Sally is. She could be ____________.
7 Do you want a place to relax on your holiday? There's ____________ better than here!
8 It's so noisy. Let's go ____________ quieter.

4 Complete these sentences so that they are true for you.

1 Everyone knows that I ______________________.
2 For my next holiday I'd like to go somewhere ______________________.
3 I don't like eating anything that has got ______________________ in it.
4 I think anyone can learn to ______________________.

→ workbook page 36

VOCABULARY
IT terms

5 Match the phrases with the meanings. Write numbers 1–10.

1 to key in your password | **2** to install a program
3 to attach a file | **4** to have network coverage
5 to upload a photo | **6** to delete a message
7 ~~to open an attachment~~ | **8** to buy an app
9 to activate flight mode | **10** to download a file

a to click on the icon of a file that comes with an email [7]
b to have a signal that lets you make phone calls, etc. [ ]
c to add a separate element (e.g. a photo, a document, a video) to an email [ ]
d to make an image available on the internet [ ]
e to pay for a program for your mobile or tablet [ ]
f to type a secret word that gives you access to a computer or a website [ ]
g to put a program on a computer [ ]
h to switch on a function on your mobile or tablet so you can't go online [ ]
i to remove a piece of text so it cannot be seen any more [ ]
j to copy information or a program from the internet onto your computer hard disk [ ]

6 SPEAKING **Work in pairs. Ask and answer these questions.**

1 How many different ways do you have to go online?
2 How often do you post something on social media?
3 What kind of things do you usually post?
4 What ways do you know of keeping passwords secure but remembering them?

7 Draw spider diagrams for these verbs.

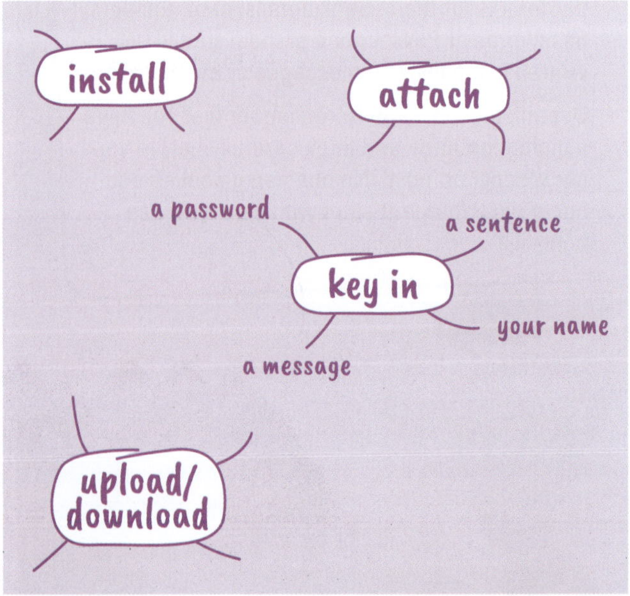

→ workbook page 38

LISTENING

8 Match the words and phrases with the meanings. Write the numbers 1–6 in the boxes.

1 to fall for a scam | **2** personal data
3 phishing | **4** identity theft
5 a pop-up | **6** a PIN

a a secret number you use with your bank card ☐
b information about you and your life ☐
c a new window or message that appears on your computer screen ☐
d when people try to get you to give information over the internet ☐
e to not understand when someone tries to get money from you with lies ☐
f to steal information about someone, then pretend to be them ☐

9 SPEAKING **Work in pairs. Answer the questions.**

1 Which of the things in Exercise 8 did you already know about?
2 Do you know anyone who has had problems because they sent personal data to someone else?

10 4.02 **Listen to Mark and his dad. Answer the questions.**

1 Why is Mark's dad angry?
2 What does he want Mark not to do?

11 4.02 **Listen again. Look at the six sentences. Mark them T (true) or F (false). Then correct the false ones.**

1 Mark's grandfather didn't lose much money.
2 Mark doesn't think he will fall for a scam.
3 Identity theft is less of a problem now than before.
4 Mark got an email offering him a new laptop.
5 The brother of one of Mark's friends lost money.
6 Mark's dad thinks only teenagers are tricked online.

GRAMMAR
all / some / none / any of them

12 Complete the sentences. Look back at the article on page 39 to check.

The apps you use, the emails you send, everything you've searched for – [0] *all of them* are part of your digital footprint

There are plenty of people looking at information about you, and [1] ______ want to steal from you.

Bank details, card numbers, passwords or PINs – [2] ______ should be written in emails.

13 Complete the rule with *things* / *more* / *none*.

RULE: We use the expressions ***all*** / ***some*** / [1] ______ / ***any of them*** to refer back to a group (of [2] ______ or people) and say [3] ______ about it.

14 Choose the correct words.

1 My friends had a great time at my birthday party. *All* / *None* of them wanted to leave!
2 Which of these pens is Carla's? They all look exactly the same, so *any* / *some* of them could be hers.
3 These bikes all look good, but I'm sure *some* / *any* of them are better than others.
4 These T-shirts are really cool. *None* / *Any* of them would be fine for me.
5 These caps weren't expensive. I got *all* / *none* of them for £12.
6 I tried on lots of different jeans, but *none* / *some* of them were the right size for me.
7 All the questions were really hard – I couldn't answer *none* / *any* of them!
8 Her songs are OK – I quite like *some* / *any* of them.

15 Complete the sentences with *all* / *some* / *none* / *any*. (There may be more than one possible answer.)

1 There are 32 students in Sarah's class. It's amazing that *all* of them like music, but ______ of them listen to jazz.
2 I like most American TV shows, but ______ of them are terrible!
3 OK, he scored three goals – but ______ of them were lucky!
4 The cakes that I made were horrible – we couldn't eat ______ of them, so we threw them all away.
5 My three brothers like IT, but ______ of them is as good with computers as my sister.
6 Look at those cameras. ______ of them are very cheap, but others are very expensive.

→ workbook page 36

READING

1 Look at the messages. Match them with the types of communication in the list. Write a–e in the boxes.

1 email ☐
2 message on a messaging app ☐
3 post on an advertisement website ☐
4 social media post ☐
5 text message ☐

2 🔊 4.03 Read and listen to the messages and choose the correct answers.

1 Why does Billy apologise to his brother Sam?
   A He wants to buy another guitar.
   B He has dreams that may not come true.
   C He won't be home in time to make dinner.
2 What's the purpose of Gemma's message (a)?
   A To invite Billy to her house on Sunday
   B To tell Billy she's not a good guitarist
   C To ask Billy if he can play a song
3 In her post (b), Gemma
   A says she learned something new.
   B tells people she had a good time with Billy.
   C says that Billy's a good guitar player.
4 In her post (c), Gemma says the guitar
   A is new and is in OK condition.
   B is an acoustic guitar.
   C comes in a case which costs extra.
5 Billy writes an email (d)
   A to suggest that he and Gemma play guitar together again.
   B to say he wants to buy her guitar.
   C to say he knows some good videos on YouTube.
6 In his message (e), Billy says that he
   A doesn't like Neil Young's music.
   B liked the guitar practice, but not the tea.
   C hopes they can play together again.

Train to THINK

Logical sequencing

3 Read the messages again. Work out a logical order. Write letters a–e in the right order.

☐ 1 ☐ 2 ☐ 3 ☐ 4 ☐ 5

4 SPEAKING Work in pairs. Compare your ideas and discuss any differences.

Hi Sam,
You know I want a better guitar. Well, my friend Jake told me that his friend is selling one, so I'm going to check it out this evening. I'm going to be really late back. So sorry – you'd better make your own dinner tonight. When your brother is a big star, he'll buy you dinner every night. ☺

Billy Smith

a

Hey Billy. I'm not doing anything on Sunday. Want to come round? I've been practising a song called *Heart of Gold* – do you know it? Maybe we could play together? To be honest, I'm not very good at the guitar. How about you? Gemma

Gemma Black

b

Gemma Black

Great fun yesterday. A new friend came round and we played guitar together. He's a beginner, but I'm not great, so we had fun. We watched a YouTube lesson for a song called *Heart of Gold* – it's not too difficult to play. We had tea together afterwards, too.

c

Sign in | Post

Hi everyone, I've got an acoustic guitar that I want to sell. It's a two-year-old Yamaha, perfect condition, £250 with the case. Anyone interested? If not, tell your friends please!

d

To: Gemma
From: billy@thinkmail.com

Hi!

Hi Gemma,
I've thought about the guitar. It's really nice but a bit more than I can really afford, so I'm going to stick with my old one for now.
But it was nice to talk. Thanks for the tip about the YouTube lessons – that guy is much better than the one I've been using. You know, we ought to practise together some time. What do you think?
Billy

e

MESSAGES
Contacts

Hi G,
Thanks for last Sunday. It was fun playing the guitar with you and the tea was nice, too. I've listened to some more songs by Neil Young. Old guy, but cool tunes! We should do it again soon.
B
PS Love the photo on Instagram!

GRAMMAR
should(n't), had better, ought to

5 **Complete these sentences from the messages on page 42. Then choose the correct words to complete the rules.**

1 You ______ make your own dinner tonight.
2 We ______ do it again soon.
3 We ______ practise together some time.

> RULE: ***Should***, ***had better*** and ***ought to*** are used to give [4]**advice / information**.
> - ***Should*** and ***ought to*** mean more or less the same, but we usually don't use ***ought to*** in questions and negative statements.
> - The meaning of ***had better*** is often a little stronger. The speaker wants to say that there are [5]**positive / negative** consequences if you ignore the advice.
>
> These verbs [6]**do / don't** use an auxiliary verb in the negative: ***shouldn't***, ***oughtn't to***, ***had better not***.

6 **Match the questions to the answers. Write a–g in the boxes. Choose the correct word in each answer.**

1 I've broken my friend's watch. What should I do? ☐
2 I've got toothache. What should I do? ☐
3 I didn't do very well in the test. What should I do? ☐
4 I'd like to go climbing, but I've never done it before. What should I do? ☐
5 I got an email from someone, asking me to send them money. Should I reply to it? ☐
6 I'm angry with my brother. He said something I didn't like. What should I do? ☐
7 This sweater my sister gave me looks terrible. I don't like it at all. What should I do? ☐

a You *should* / *shouldn't* respond. It could be a scam.
b You *should* / *shouldn't* tell him. It's best to be honest with him.
c You'd *better* / *better not* return it to the shop. That would really hurt her feelings.
d You *shouldn't* / *ought to* go back and study everything again.
e You'd *better* / *shouldn't* get some training. It can be dangerous.
f You *ought to* / *shouldn't* see a dentist.
g You'd *better* / *shouldn't* say sorry the next time you see your friend.

7 **Look at these pictures. Write short dialogues with (serious or funny) answers giving advice.**

1 *What should I do?*
You should run after the man and give him his wallet.

→ workbook page 37

VOCABULARY
Language for giving advice

8 **Look at the phrases below and answer the questions.**

to give (bad / good / practical / useful) advice about [something]
to take / follow [someone's] advice
to ignore [someone's] advice
to advise [someone][to do something]
to advise against [something]
to be advisable

a What's the difference between *advice* and *advise*?
b Which of the phrases mean(s)
– not to listen to somebody's advice?
– do what somebody has advised you to do?
c How do you say 'advisable' in your language?

9 **Complete the sentences with phrases from Exercise 8. Use the correct verb forms.**

1 I've told Peter he shouldn't post photos like that, but he has always ______ my ______ .
2 Should I buy a tablet or a laptop? Can you give me some ______ what's better?
3 He wants to become a web designer. His dad has ______ him to take a course. He should ______ that ______ .
4 My uncle has a heart problem. This web page ______ fatty foods.

→ workbook page 38

FUNCTIONS
Giving advice

10 SPEAKING **Ask and answer questions with a partner.**

1 Imagine you meet somebody who has never used a computer. What advice would you give them about social networking?
2 Are you good at giving advice? Say why (not) and give examples.
3 When do you find it difficult to follow someone's advice?

THINK

The evolution of writing

Culture

1 **Look at the photos. What do they show?**

FROM CAVES TO KINDLES – HOW READING HAS CHANGED

1 ☐

Cave paintings are the oldest pictures. Some of them, like the beautiful images in the caves of Altamira in the north of Spain, are almost 30,000 years old. Many of these paintings show animals or hunting scenes. The images do not have written words, but when we look at them, we get an idea of the emotions the people felt when drawing them. The paintings tell stories of hopes and fears. They are an early form of communication.

2 ☐

Sometime between 4000 and 3000 BCE, people in Egypt and Mesopotamia developed the skill of writing. They engraved text on stone tablets first. But it was impossible to carry stones from place to place. The invention of papyrus allowed documents to be moved easily. Writing on papyrus made it easier to correct mistakes, too. And do you know how they did that? When a scribe – the person who wrote the documents – made a mistake, they licked the ink off the papyrus before it got dry and made their corrections!

3 ☐

People made the first books from papyrus and from thin animal skins. Paper was invented in China as early as 105 CE. The quality of paper soon became very good. The world's oldest known printed book is from China, too. It was published on May 11, 868 CE. In Europe, books were written manually until the middle of the 15th century, when Johannes Gutenberg invented the printing press in Germany. Since that time, almost 140 million books have been published worldwide. For many people, one of life's greatest pleasures is spending a few hours in a bookshop browsing through the books.

4 ☐

Books will be around for many years, of course. But there are many other ways of reading books and magazines, such as e-books and apps on mobile phones, which allow you to buy and download reading material to carry around with you and read whenever and wherever you want to.

2 **Read the article quickly. Match the paragraph headings with the paragraphs. Write the letters a–f. There are two headings you don't need.**

- **a** The invention of books by Gutenberg
- **b** Early forms of written communication
- **c** Books in their most modern form
- **d** From stone tablets to the printing press
- **e** Communication without reading and writing
- **f** The history of bookmaking

3 4.04 **Read and listen to the article and check your answers in Exercise 2.**

4 SPEAKING **Work in pairs. Discuss the questions.**

1. How important are books for you? Give reasons.
2. What book(s) have you read recently? Did you like it / them?
3. Do you prefer printed books or e-books? Why?

PRONUNCIATION

The short /ʌ/ vowel sound Go to page 120.

5 **VOCABULARY** **There are eight highlighted words in the article. Match the words with these meanings. Write the words.**

0 a large hole in a cliff or mountain that goes inside *cave*
1 paper made from plants ______
2 looking through a book or magazine, without reading everything ______
3 happiness, love and anger ______
4 produced (and sold) a book ______
5 moved the tongue across something ______
6 words that are cut into stone ______
7 a machine to make newspapers, books or magazines ______

WRITING
A web page giving advice

1 **INPUT** **Read this information and decide who it would be important for. Then answer the questions.**

1 Where do people use public computers?
2 What other examples not mentioned in the text can you think of?
3 Why should you never save a password on a public computer?
4 What's the problem with just closing the browser when you want to finish a session?

HOW TO USE A
PUBLIC COMPUTER
– SAFETY TIPS

There are times when you may want to use a public computer, for example in a hostel, a library or at an airport. That's when it's especially important to be smart and safe.

- Don't save! When you want to log into a social networking website or your email, the system will ask you, 'Do you want to save this password?' Don't click 'Yes' when you are working on a public computer.
- Log out! Make sure you do not simply close the browser when you want to leave a site. You should always log out of all sites when you finish your session.
- Close windows! If you need to walk away from the computer for any reason, you should close all the windows on the computer first. Don't leave any information on the screen that other people shouldn't see.
- Watch out! Be careful of people looking at the screen over your shoulder. Ask them politely to go somewhere else so you can use the computer in private.

2 **Rewrite the sentences by putting the words in brackets in the right position.**

1 Read our advice. (carefully)
Read our advice carefully.
2 Click 'Yes.' (don't)
3 Make you do not simply close the browser. (sure)
4 You should log out. (always)
5 Ask them to go somewhere else. (politely)

3 **Are the sentences above used to give advice or to give an opinion? Match each of them with one of the situations below. Write the numbers 1–5.**

a when the system asks you 'Do you want to save the password?' ☐
b when you want to leave a site ☐
c to be smart and safe when using public computers ☐
d if someone looks over your shoulder and watches you ☐
e when you finish your session ☐

4 **ANALYSE** **Match the content with the five sections of the text.**

Introduction	a Don't leave important information on the screen.
Bullet point 1	b Log out properly.
Bullet point 2	c Don't let people watch you.
Bullet point 3	d What is the purpose of this text?
Bullet point 4	e Don't save information.

5 **PLAN** **What would be important advice for good online behaviour? Make notes.**

Here are some ideas:
what (not) to share on social networks
creating secure passwords and how to keep them safe
what to do when you receive offensive comments on social networking websites
what you should know about uploading photos on social networks

6 **PRODUCE** **Write your text for a web page giving advice on good online behaviour (about 200 words).**

Use an introduction and bullet points to structure your text.
Use language from Exercises 2 and 3 to give advice, and make sure your readers understand what situations your advice refers to.

B1 Preliminary for Schools

READING
Part 2: Matching

→ workbook page 43

1 **For each question, choose the correct answer. The young people below are looking for a film to watch. Look at the eight film reviews. Decide which film would be most suitable for the people below.**

1 
Dawn loves thinking about the future and how human society will be different. She's a fan of films that are set in a time many years from now but doesn't really enjoy films that are too frightening.

2 
Paula's job is very boring so when she gets home she likes watching films with special effects, but she's not a fan of sci-fi. She also likes films with fast action.

3 
Keith is a romantic guy who enjoys a good love story but it must have a happy ending. He doesn't like serious films very much, and likes to have a laugh, too.

4 
Lisa's not really a fan of fiction and only watches films about real life. She's interested in anything from history to nature to science, as long as she learns something from it.

5 
Graham likes many different kinds of films, but cartoons are his favourite. He especially likes them when they are based on a true story, especially on historical events.

HOT NEW FILMS

A THE INVISIBLE WORLD
Using the most advanced camera technology in the world, this documentary takes us to places that have never been filmed before. From deep under the sea to inside the human body, this film contains some of the most amazing images you will ever see.

B THE KING WHO NEVER WAS
In 1936 Edward VIII decided to give up being king after less than a year so he could be with the woman he loved. This film revisits one of the most popular 'royal stories' of all time and mixes fact and fiction to create an interesting drama. It will keep audiences entertained.

C IT COULD HAPPEN TO YOU
Imagine waking up in the future in a house that is not the house you went to sleep in. Imagine not recognising your children – even though they all seem to think you are their mum. This fascinating sci-fi takes us to a world where people buy and sell memories.

D WILL THEY? WON'T THEY?
Ever since school, Jack and Jill have been best friends. But now they are in their twenties, and their feelings are changing. Is either of them brave enough to see that they are falling in love? Will they do something about it? Of course, it is all OK in the end in this likeable rom com.

E JOAN OF ARC
The well-known story of the young French woman who fought and died for the freedom of her country, back in the 15th century. Her fantastic story is told in a very emotional way in this animated version, with the voices of many famous film stars. It is also a historically accurate account. Young children might find it disturbing.

F TOMORROW NOW
The year is 2080 and for the last ten years Earth has been in contact with aliens. Today is the day that we finally welcome them to our planet. How will they change our lives and are they really as friendly as they seem? One of the scariest films you will see this year.

G COUNTDOWN TO DISASTER
A speeding train is going to crash into a nuclear power station and no one can stop it. Or can they? Special agent Ryan has got an hour to stop the disaster, but there's a problem – he has a bomb tied around his waist. Car chases, explosions and amazing special effects – this thriller has got it all.

H OLIVER TWIST
This wonderful version of the famous Charles Dickens story will be enjoyed by everyone. An animated cartoon, it takes us back to Victorian London and wonderful characters like Oliver himself, The Artful Dodger and Fagin. There have not been many better animated fiction films in the past twenty years.

WRITING
Part 2: An article or story

→ workbook page 107

2 **Choose one of these questions. Write your answer in about 100 words.**

Question 1

- Your English teacher has asked you to write a story.
- Your story must begin with this sentence.
  I had tickets to see my favourite band and I was very excited.
- Write your **story**.

Question 2

- You see this notice in an international English-language magazine.
- Write your **article**.

ARTICLES WANTED!
USING LESS ENERGY

What things in your everyday life do you use energy to do?
What can you do to reduce the amount of energy you use?
Why is it important to save energy?
Tell us what you think.
Write an article about these questions and we will publish the most interesting in our magazine.

VOCABULARY

1 Complete the sentences with the words in the list. There are two extra words.

advice | advise | attachment | comedy | documentary | download | ignore | key | mode | news | thriller | upload

1 If you're on a plane, don't forget to put your mobile phone in flight ________________ .
2 There was a ________________ programme on TV last night – I've never laughed so much in my life!
3 You need to fill in a form. You can ________________ it from our website.
4 There was an interesting programme last night – a ________________ about the history of my country.
5 Let me give you some ________________ . Don't go to that new café, it's awful.
6 My father always watches the ________________ on TV to see what's happening in the world.
7 I'm sure you think it's a good idea, but I'd ________________ against it, to be honest.
8 I got your email but you forgot to send the ________________ with it. Can you send it, please?
9 The first thing I do when I switch my computer on is ________________ in my password.
10 He doesn't know what he's talking about, so you should just ________________ his advice!

/10

GRAMMAR

2 Complete the sentences with the words in the list.

best | better | everyone | no one | none | someone

1 I advertised my bike for sale, but ________________ wanted it.
2 This place makes the ________________ hamburgers I've ever eaten.
3 I've got a problem and I need to talk to ________________ , please.
4 I asked all my friends, but ________________ of them knew the answer.
5 I think her new film is ________________ than her last one.
6 The school trip was wonderful. ________________ had a really good time.

3 Find and correct the mistake in each sentence.

1 Grandad looks really tired. I think we ought go home now.
2 The film isn't as good than the book.
3 There were four football matches on TV last night, and all of them was brilliant!
4 It's the most bad party I've ever been to.
5 He talks more quiet than his brother.
6 She's really angry. We'd better to go and say sorry.

/12

FUNCTIONAL LANGUAGE

4 Complete the mini-dialogues with the words in the list.

against | everything | hand | help | ought | should | with | would

1 A Is ________________ OK?
B Yes, thanks. But perhaps I ________________ take an aspirin.
2 A Can I ________________ you at all?
B Well, yes, that ________________ be great. Thanks!
3 A Could you help me ________________ something? I want to send money to someone who wrote me an email.
B Well, you know, that's not a good idea. I'd advise ________________ it.
4 A Joe? This is heavy. Can you lend me a ________________ ?
B Hmm, it looks too heavy. You ________________ to use a machine.

/8

MY SCORE /30

22–30 | 10–21 | 0–9

5 MUSIC TO MY EARS

Get THINKING

Watch the video and think: how do you listen to music?

OBJECTIVES

FUNCTIONS: asking about feelings; making helpful suggestions

GRAMMAR: present perfect continuous; present perfect simple vs. present perfect continuous

VOCABULARY: making music; musical instruments; phrases with *out*

1 ______________

2 ______________

3 ______________

4 ______________

5 ______________

6 ______________

READING

1 5.01 **Listen. What type of music do you hear? Write the words under the pictures.**

dance music | jazz | opera | pop | rap | rock

2 **What other types of music can you think of?**

3 SPEAKING **Work in pairs. What kind of music do you like? Ask and answer questions.**

Do you like ... ?

I love/like/can't stand ...

I've never listened to ...

4 **Look at the photos on the next page and answer the questions.**

1 Who are the people?

2 What do you think the connection between the photos is?

5 **Read the article quickly and check your ideas.**

6 5.02 **Read and listen to the article again and answer the questions.**

1 What type of music did Sheku play at the royal wedding?

2 How many people watched him play at the wedding?

3 When and where did Sheku first play in front of the prince?

4 How did Sheku announce he was playing at the wedding?

5 Where did Sheku study music?

6 Who did Sheku perform with on a talent show?

7 Why was he offered a record contract?

8 How successful was *Inspiration*?

A BRIGHT STAR

On Saturday May 19th 2018, millions of people around the world watched as Prince Harry married the American actress Meghan Markle at St George's Chapel in Windsor Castle, in front of 600 guests. As they signed the marriage register, a young cellist played three pieces of classical music.

It was a dream come true for 19-year-old Sheku Kanneh-Mason. It was the biggest performance of his short professional career so far, and a sign that he was quickly becoming one of the most admired classical musicians in the world.

This wasn't Sheku's first performance in front of the prince. A year earlier Harry was in the audience for a charity concert in London. Perhaps it was Sheku's performance at this concert that resulted in his royal invitation. The following April an excited Sheku announced on Twitter that Meghan had phoned him to see if he would like to play at the wedding.

Sheku has been playing the cello since he was six. He is one of seven children in an amazingly talented family from Nottingham in England. Sheku and his six brothers and sisters are all extremely talented classical musicians. His eldest sister, Isata, won a scholarship to the famous Royal Academy of Music in London to study the piano. A few years later, Sheku followed her when he gained a place at the same institution to study the cello. He was only nine years old. He has been performing with Isata and his older brother Braimah for many years. In 2015 they decided to enter the talent show *Britain's Got Talent* as the Kanneh-Masons. Their performances on the show were watched by several million people and they reached the semi-finals.

A year later Sheku entered the BBC Young Musician of the Year competition, which he won. He became the first black musician ever to win the award. He was just 17 years old. As a result of this success he also got a contract with the music publishing company Decca to record an album.

In 2018, he released his first album, *Inspiration*. The album spent four weeks in the UK top 40 charts and it contains many famous classical pieces. Sheku also includes classical versions of songs by Bob Marley and Leonard Cohen on the album. It has introduced a younger audience to classical music.

The future is looking bright for Sheku Kanneh-Mason!

TH!NK values

Following your dreams

7 Match these people with their dreams.

1 Jessie is a really good artist. ☐
2 Kylie loves acting. ☐
3 David is great at football. ☐
4 Lance has written a book. ☐

a 'I want to get it published.'
b 'I want to be in a play.'
c 'I want to play professionally.'
d 'I'd love to have an exhibition of my work.'

8 What should the people in Exercise 7 do to realise their dreams? Give advice. Make notes for each one.

David / join club

9 SPEAKING Work in pairs. Compare your ideas.

10 SPEAKING Discuss these questions in small groups.

1 What is your dream?
2 What can you do to make it come true?

GRAMMAR
Present perfect continuous

1 Complete the sentences with the correct form of the words in brackets. Check your answers in the article on page 49.

1 Sheku ________________ (play) the cello since he was six.
2 He ________________ (perform) with Isata and his older brother Braimah for many years.

2 Match the example sentences below with the rules. Write the numbers 1–3.

1 I've been learning the piano for two years.
2 I've been practising the piano since 10 am.
3 I've been playing the piano all day and I'm tired now.

> **RULE:** The present perfect continuous is used for actions happening over a period of time. We use it to:
> a emphasise how long an activity has been happening. The activity may or may not be complete. ☐
> b talk generally about situations or activities that started in the past and are still continuing now. ☐
> c talk about situations or activities that have stopped but have a result in the present. ☐

3 Choose the correct words.

1 He's been *talking* / *talked* on the phone all morning.
2 I've *being* / *been* playing this game for hours now.
3 Jo *hasn't* / *haven't* been feeling well for a few days.
4 They've *been* / *being* studying since ten o'clock.
5 We *haven't* / *hasn't* been living here for very long.
6 The dog's been *barked* / *barking* for half an hour.

4 Complete the sentences. Use the correct form of the words and *for* or *since*.

1 We're tired because we ________________ (run) __________ hours.
2 I ________________ (wait) for her __________ 40 minutes!
3 He ________________ (watch) TV __________ 9 am.
4 She's red because she ________________ (lie) in the sun __________ this morning.
5 They ________________ (walk) in the rain __________ an hour and they're really wet.
6 Dad's exhausted because he ________________ (work) in the garden __________ he got up.

5 SPEAKING Work in pairs. Find out how long your partner has been doing these things.

1 living in their house
2 learning English
3 going to school
4 talking

How long have you been learning English?

For two years.

→ workbook page 46

PRONUNCIATION
been: strong /biːn/ and weak /bɪn/
Go to page 120.

VOCABULARY
Making music

6 Complete the story of Dymonde with the verbs in the list.

enter | entered | going | playing | record | released | start | streaming | won | writing

Alana Bolan started out as a teacher, but she always wanted to be a musician and she always loved [1]______ *music* and *lyrics* for songs. One day she decided to [2]______ *a band*, so she put an advert online. She soon found the band mates she was looking for. They called themselves Dymonde. They practised hard and started [3]______ *local gigs*. A few months ago they decided to [4]______ *a talent show*. They [5]______ *the competition*, and their prize was a day in a recording studio. They used it to [6]______ *a single* called *New Love*. They [7]______ *the single* a week ago, and loads of people have been [8]______ *it*. It's already [9]______ *the charts*. Radio stations have been playing it lots, too. Next month their album is coming out and they are [10]______ *on tour* all over the country. Get your tickets fast! They are running out quickly.

7 SPEAKING Work in pairs. Ask your partner about their favourite band. Use the expressions in Exercise 6.

Who writes the songs?

Have you been to any of their gigs?

→ workbook page 48

WRITING
The story of your favourite band

8 Write the story of your favourite band.

Write about:

- how they started.
- how long they have been together.
- how long you have liked them and why.

LISTENING

9 5.05 **Listen to the interview with Dana. What is she talking about?**

10 5.05 **Listen again and answer the questions.**

1 How important is music for Dana?
2 What instrument would Dana like to play?
3 What music does Dana listen to when she's studying?
4 What does Dana think about song lyrics?

11 5.06 **Now listen to Ben answering the same questions. Write three things he has in common with Dana.**

1 ______
2 ______
3 ______

SPEAKING

12 Work in pairs. Do the quiz. Then discuss your answers to these questions.

- Do you agree or disagree with your score? Why?
- What music do you listen to when you are sad?
- What songs have special memories for you?
- What are your favourite song lyrics?
- How do you choose what music to listen to?
- What music do your friends like?

WordWise: Phrasal verbs with *out*

13 Complete each of these sentences from the unit so far with a word from the list.

coming | find | go | running | sort | started

1 Alana Bolan ______ out as a teacher.
2 Next month their album is ______ out.
3 Hurry up and get your tickets. They are ______ out quickly.
4 When I've got a problem to ______ out, listening to classical music can help.
5 I'd never ______ out and buy any music.
6 ______ out just how music mad you are.

14 Match the phrases and the meanings.

1 to start out ___
2 to find out ___
3 to go out ___
4 to come out ___
5 to run out ___
6 to sort out ___

a to discover
b to begin your working life
c to leave your house
d to become available
e to find an answer or solution to a problem
f to finish, use or sell all of something, so that there is none left

15 Complete the sentences with the correct form of the verbs in Exercise 14.

1 John isn't here. He ______ about 20 minutes ago.
2 It's a really old film. I think it ______ in 2005.
3 We need to go to the supermarket – we ______ of milk.
4 The police are trying to ______ who started the trouble last night.
5 We had some problems with the computer, but we ______ them ______ yesterday.
6 She's a famous singer now, but she ______ as a dancer.

→ workbook page 48

DOES MUSIC ROCK YOUR WORLD?

COULD YOU LIVE WITHOUT IT?

Take our quiz and find out just how important music is in your life.

For each question, choose the sentence that describes you best. Then work out your score and find out just how music mad you are.

1
A I only listen to music when I'm happy. ☐
B Music makes me feel better when I'm feeling down. ☐
C I listen to different music depending on how I feel. ☐

2
A I have loads of memories connected to different songs. ☐
B I never listen to music from when I was younger. ☐
C I get bored with songs quickly. ☐

3
A My musical taste influences the clothes I wear. ☐
B Music has nothing to do with fashion. ☐
C I don't really think about what I wear. ☐

4
A I have the same musical tastes as my best friends. ☐
B I like different music from most of my friends. ☐
C I always know if I'm going to be friends with someone when they tell me their taste in music. ☐

5
A I always listen to the lyrics in songs. ☐
B Melody is more important than lyrics. ☐
C Melody and lyrics are both really important in a song. ☐

GO TO PAGE 127 TO FIND OUT YOUR SCORE!

READING

1 SPEAKING **Work in pairs. Make a list of advantages and disadvantages of listening to live music compared to listening to recorded music.**

Advantages	***Disadvantages***
More exciting	*It's expensive*

2 **Read the article quickly. Which band is thinking of using holograms on stage?**

THE FUTURE OF LIVE MUSIC

Technology has always played an important part in the development of pop music – from the instruments that the bands play and the live shows that they perform to the way we listen to music in our homes or on the move. But advances in technology over the next few years are promising to bring even bigger changes.

HOLOGRAMS

For around 50 years, people of all ages have been enjoying ABBA's music. They have played almost 100 international concerts, but since 1982, when the band played their last show, fans have had little hope of ever seeing their favourite group live on stage again. That is now about to change as the band have announced plans for their first shows in nearly forty years. Bands from the 70s and 80s playing together again is nothing new, but it is no surprise that a band as big as ABBA are planning to do things a little bit differently. The four members of the band will not be on the stage together. Instead, they will appear as holograms. The holograms will show the band as they looked back in 1979, when ABBA were the biggest band in the world. And they won't be the only band to have returned to the stage via holograms. In 2018 Freddie Mercury appeared in hologram form alongside Queen in Las Vegas, even though he died more than 25 years ago.

VIRTUAL REALITY (VR)

VR technology has made lots of progress recently. You may soon be able to enjoy watching your favourite band live without even leaving your house. Developers have been making plans to launch a new app that will allow fans to watch live concerts that are being streamed directly to VR headsets. Not only will you be able to watch the band from the crowd, but you will also have the possibility of watching the show on stage with the band. And all of this will cost you about a tenth of the ticket price for the venue. These advances in technology are very exciting, but do fans really want to watch a show knowing that their musical heroes aren't really there? And can watching through a VR headset ever really match up to the experience of actually being there? Is the latest technology really always the best? Perhaps we should look at the case of vinyl. Who would have thought that a format that was replaced by the CD, then downloading and, finally, streaming, would have made such a big return. Perhaps sometimes the old-fashioned ways of doing things might just be better.

3 5.07 **Read and listen to the article again. Answer the questions.**

1 Which sentence best describes ABBA's popularity?
   - A They are mainly liked by older people.
   - B They are more popular now than they were fifty years ago.
   - C They have been successful for half a century.
   - D They were forgotten for quite a few years.

2 How will ABBA's new shows be different?
   - A The band won't be there on stage.
   - B They will play mainly new songs.
   - C They will all be a lot older.
   - D The audiences will be mainly young people.

3 Why might watching a concert using Virtual Reality be considered better than going to a venue?
   - A Most people already have the technology in their homes.
   - B It allows you to watch from different places in the venue.
   - C You can play with the band on stage.
   - D It costs 50% less.

4 What is the writer's conclusion about technology and music at the end of the text?
   - A Technology can be used to bring people what they want.
   - B There's nothing we can do to stop new technology from taking over.
   - C We should always be looking for better ways of doing things.
   - D It might not always be true to say that new is better.

GRAMMAR

Present perfect simple vs. present perfect continuous

4 Look at the article on page 52 to complete the sentences. Then complete the rules and match them with the example sentences.

1 For around 50 years, people ______ enjoying ABBA's music.
2 They ______ almost 100 international concerts.

RULE:
- Use the present perfect [3]______ to talk about an action that is not finished. ☐
- Use the present perfect [4]______ to stress the *finished result* of a completed activity and the *amount* completed. ☐

5 Complete the sentences with the phrases in the list.

's been taking | 've been preparing | 've been watching
've eaten | hasn't taken | 've played
've been playing | 's been writing | 's written | 've made

1 Sarah ______________ more than 200 poems.
She ______________ poems since she was eight.
2 He ______________ piano lessons for three years.
He ______________ any piano exams yet.
3 I ______________ football since I was five.
I ______________ for three different teams.
4 We ______________ films all evening.
We ______________ three bags of popcorn.
5 I ______________ more than 100 cakes.
I ______________ for the party all day.

6 Complete the sentences using the correct forms of the verbs in brackets.

1 He ______________ autographs since he was ten.
He ______________ over 500. (collect)
2 Jade ______________ at Netflix for five years.
She ______________ there since 2016. (work)
3 Mum ______________ since 6 am.
She ______________ over 400 km. (drive)
4 We ______________ for an hour.
We ______________ more than 2 km! (swim)
5 Tom ______________ more than 2,000 children.
He ______________ since he was 22. (teach)
6 They ______________ apples all day.
They ______________ hundreds! (pick)

→ workbook page 47

VOCABULARY

Musical instruments

7 Write the instruments in the list under the pictures.

bass guitar | drums | guitar | keyboard
piano | saxophone | trumpet | violin

1

____

5

____

2

____

6

____

3

____

7

____

4

____

8

____

8 5.08 **Listen. Which instrument is playing?**

1 bass guitar

→ workbook page 48

SPEAKING

9 Work in pairs. Answer the questions.

1 Do you play an instrument? If yes, how long have you been playing it? If no, would you like to learn to play one?
2 Which of the instruments in Exercise 7 do you really like? Which instruments don't you like?
3 What famous musicians can you think of? How long have they been playing music? Have you seen them playing live?

1 5.09 **Look at the photos. Why does the boy look unhappy? Listen and read to check.**

Laura: Tom! Hi! Here you are, looking in the music shop window. Why am I not surprised!?
Tom: Oh, hi Laura. You OK?
Laura: Well, I'm fine. But you don't look very happy. What's up?
Tom: Nothing.
Laura: Oh, come on. What's the matter?
Tom: Well, I'm just a bit upset. Look. There's that keyboard, the one I've always wanted, 25% off. Down to £240. And I still can't afford it.
Laura: Oh, I see. But you've been saving for ages, haven't you?
Tom: Yes, and I've saved £150. But it's not enough, is it? Even with 25% off, I still need another £90.
Laura: Can't you ask your parents to help? Can they lend you some money?
Tom: No way. They've just bought a car. They haven't got any spare money at the moment.
Laura: Tell me about it. I asked my parents to lend me some money the other day. They were nice about it, but they said no. They're saving to go to Canada to see my uncle.
Tom: OK, there's no point in standing here looking in the window. I'll just have to forget about it for now. Let's go.
Laura: Well, if you say so. What a shame.
Man: Hello! Looking at the keyboards? Come in and have a look. You can try one if you want.
Tom: Thanks, but no thanks. I can't afford the one I want. That black one, the Condor.
Man: That one? I've got another one in the shop. It's got a scratch on it, so I'm thinking of taking another £100 off the price. Interested?
Tom: Absolutely! I can't wait to see it!
Laura: Come on, Tom, let's go in!

2 Read the dialogue again and answer the questions.

1 How much money has Tom saved?
2 How much more does he need to buy the keyboard he wants?
3 Why won't Tom's parents be able to lend him any money?
4 Why is the shop-owner going to reduce the price of one keyboard by another £100?

3 SPEAKING **Think of Tom's situation. Look at the statements below and discuss in pairs.**

1 Would you save up for a more expensive keyboard model or buy a cheaper one with the money you have got?
2 Would you buy a damaged product if it is cheaper/ reduced in price?

Phrases for fluency

4 Find the underlined expressions in the dialogue and use them to complete the conversations.

1 **A** Hey Mandy. [1]______________________?
B I'm tired! I had problems with the homework last night.
A [2]______________________! I took four hours to finish it! And I think I got some things wrong.
B Me, too. Oh well. [3]______________________ worrying about it. Let's give it to the teacher and see.

2 **A** The Cup Final's on TV tonight. [4]______________________!
B I know. It's really exciting. Do you want to come and watch it with me at my house?
A [5]______________________! Your television's terrible.
B Well, [6]______________________. But I think our TV's really good.

FUNCTIONS
Asking about feelings

KEY LANGUAGE

1 What's up? 3 How are you feeling?
2 Is something the matter? 4 Are you OK?

5 Match these answers to the questions in the Key Language box.

a Not great. ___
b Yes, I'm fine. ___
c Nothing. ___
d I'm just a bit upset. ___

6 SPEAKING **When you feel upset, what other things can people do to help you feel better? Discuss in pairs.**

ROLE PLAY **Helpful suggestions**

Work in pairs. Student A: go to page 127. Student B: go to page 128. Look at the role cards and do the role play.

LIFE COMPETENCIES

Learning to manage your money is an important skill to develop. By planning what you spend, you can buy the things you need and not waste your money on things that aren't important.

1 ▶ 15 **Watch the video. Summarise Anna's advice about money in one sentence.**

2 ▶ 15 **Watch again and complete the sayings.**

1 ______ doesn't grow on ______ .
2 You can't have your ______ and ______ it, too.
3 A ______ and his ______ are easily parted.

3 **You have £80 for the week. How will you spend it? For each question, choose an option. Add up your answers and make sure you have enough money!**

1 Computer games
- Play the games you have – free
- Buy a second-hand game – £20
- Buy a brand-new game – £50

2 Clothes
- Wear what you have – free
- Buy something second-hand – £20
- Buy something new – £50

3 Food
- Eat at home – free
- Buy some snacks at school – £10
- Go for a meal with your friends – £20

4 Mobile phone
- Don't use any data or make any calls – free
- Get a cheap plan with some data – £5
- Get a plan with unlimited calls and data – £15

5 Saving money
- Don't save any money – £0
- Save £10
- Save £30

4 SPEAKING **Compare your spending choices with a partner. Explain how you made your decisions.**

5 **Complete your choices again, but this time you have £40. Was it more difficult?**

6 SPEAKING **Discuss these questions with your partner.**

1 Are you saving money at the moment? What for?
2 What do you do when you have no money?
3 Do you have a spending plan?
4 If you don't, do you think it might be useful to have one?

Me and my world

7 **Look at the pie chart. What percentage of their money does this person save?**

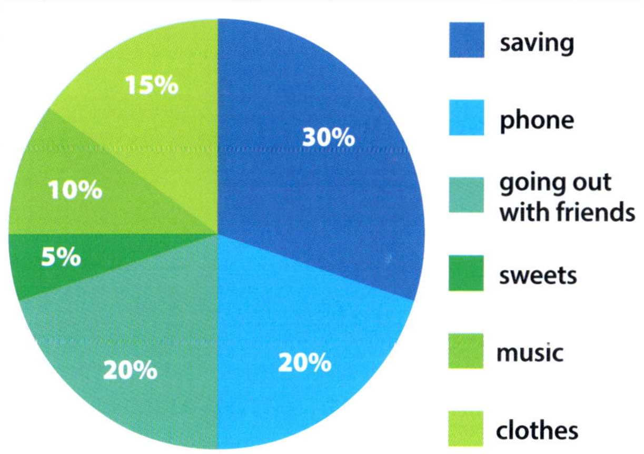

8 SPEAKING **Draw a pie chart for how you spend your money. Then work with a partner and compare your pie charts. Are they similar or very different?**

TIPS FOR MANAGING YOUR MONEY

- Keep a spending diary and write down what you've bought each week. Then you'll be able to see what you spend your money on.
- Try to save a little bit of money each week. And when you receive lots of money at once try to save half of it. That way, you'll always have money when you need it.
- Open a bank account. It's easier to know how much you have saved, and harder to waste money, if you don't have the cash on you.

6 NO PLANET B

Get THINKING

Watch the video and think: do you use a lot of plastic?

▶16

OBJECTIVES

FUNCTIONS: expressing surprise and enthusiasm

GRAMMAR: *will (not), may (not), might (not)* for prediction; first conditional; *unless* in first conditional sentences

VOCABULARY: the environment; verbs to talk about energy

A

B

C

D

E

F

READING

1 **Match the words and phrases in the list with the photos. Write 1–6 in the boxes.**

1 a beautiful beach | **2** a dirty beach
3 clean water | **4** an attractive landscape
5 an endangered species | **6** a polluted river

2 SPEAKING **Work in pairs. Which of the above are easy / difficult / impossible to find in your town or country? Use the expressions below.**

- There is / are lots of … in …
- I think 50 years ago there were more / fewer …
- It would be good to have more …

3 SPEAKING **Tell your partner about places you have visited. Which of the things in Exercise 1 did you see?**

Years ago I visited …

I saw lots of …

I was surprised / disappointed to see …

4 **Look at the photo on the next page. What do you think the article is about? Read the text quickly to check your ideas.**

5 6.01 **Read and listen to the article again. Mark the sentences T (true) or F (false).**

1 More people came to the meeting than Jackson Hinkle expected. ______
2 Team Zissou want more people to use plastic bottles. ______
3 JUST Water bottles are made of plants. ______
4 Brittany Trilford wrote a letter to world leaders. ______
5 Brittany thinks people her age are happy with world leaders. ______
6 Brittany believes that politicians should do more than they have. ______

6 SPEAKING **Work with a partner. Correct the false information in the sentences in Exercise 5.**

HOT TOPIC: SAVING THE EARTH

Many young people today are very worried about the future of the planet. This week, we look at what two teen activists are doing in their fight to save the Earth. As always, we are curious to get our readers' reactions. So tell us what you think!

Jackson Hinkle, *the US*

American teenager Jackson Hinkle and his friends invited classmates to the first meeting of an adventure club on Instagram. They thought around 30 students might come to the meeting. In fact, 300 students turned up. The group decided to set up Team Zissou Environmental Organization, and it quickly became a national movement. Their main goal is to end single-use plastics in schools and communities. Team Zissou's first campaign took place on World Water Day and they made several important promises:

We will raise money for water fountains across the school district.

We will get local businesses to stop selling single-use plastic water bottles because they cause a lot of pollution.

We will sell JUST Water in our canteens.

Jackson has learned one very important thing from his campaigning: Never give up. You must keep trying.

JUST Water comes in a paper-based bottle and has a plant-based cap. The bottle is made from 82% renewable resources, so it won't damage the environment. If sales go well in the four schools, the district might get rid of plastic water bottles and sell JUST Water in all 64 schools.

Brittany Trilford, *New Zealand*

When she was just 17, Brittany Trilford, from Wellington in New Zealand, was invited to speak to world leaders at the United Nations Conference in Rio de Janeiro, Brazil. She spoke about climate change and the need to stop talking and to act now to make real change. Brittany wants to protect the beautiful environment she lives in – an environment that will be seriously affected by climate change. She wanted world leaders to know that young people feel angry – angry because world leaders are not doing enough to protect the environment for future generations.

Her message to governments around the world is that they need to act now and think of new and better laws that may help the serious situation. Young people don't want more promises, they want action. They want to see results. Promises won't be enough.

One thing we all know now – we ARE destroying our environment. There is no Planet B, so please, let's ALL look after this one. Brittany Trilford and Jackson Hinkle have done amazing things. It's OUR turn now.

TH!NK *values*

Caring for the world

7 **Read and tick (✓) the values that are connected to the problems discussed in the article.**

1 We have responsibilities towards future generations. ☐
2 People have a right to express their opinions freely. ☐
3 All people have a right to live in peace. ☐
4 Our behaviour can make a difference. ☐
5 Humans have a responsibility to use environmentally-friendly materials. ☐
6 We must change our behaviour towards our planet. ☐

8 SPEAKING **Work in pairs. Say what you think about the values.**

I think number … is an important value.

It says … and I agree that … . Do you agree?

Yes. If we don't … , then future generations will/won't …

9 SPEAKING **Work in pairs. What environmental issues are you worried about? What do you think you could do to help?**

GRAMMAR

will (*not*), *may* (*not*), *might* (*not*) for prediction

1 Complete the examples from the article on page 57. Underline other examples of *will, won't, may* (*not*) and *might* (*not*). Then complete the rule.

1 They thought around 30 students ______ to the meeting.
2 We ______ JUST Water in our canteens.
3 Promises ______ enough.

> **RULE:** Use *will* or [4]______ to express future certainty, and [5]______ (*not*) or *might* (*not*) to express future possibility.

2 Complete the sentences. Use *will* or *won't* and the verbs in brackets.

1 I'm not exactly sure, but I think she __________ (be) home by eight o'clock at the latest.
2 I wonder if people __________ (live) on other planets in the future.
3 I'm worried about him coming with us. I'm sure he __________ (like) any of the people at the party.
4 Who do you think __________ (win) the next World Cup?
5 It's getting cloudy. Do you think it __________ (start) raining soon?
6 Oh, don't worry about my parents. I'm sure they __________ (be) angry.

3 Read the sentences and choose the correct words.

1 Don't worry, I *will* / *might* pick you up at 7.
2 The weather's a real problem. We *may* / *may not* be able to go for a walk.
3 She's not feeling well at all. She *might* / *might not* have to stay at home.
4 It *may* / *may not* be cold later, so take a jumper with you.
5 It's my dad's birthday tomorrow. My wife and I are going to visit him, so we definitely *won't* / *might not* be here.
6 I'd like to get up and watch the sunrise with you, but I *may* / *won't* just sleep instead.

4 SPEAKING Work in pairs. Think about next weekend. Talk about:

- a sport you will / won't do
- someone you may / may not see
- a film you might / might not watch

→ workbook page 54

VOCABULARY

The environment

5 Match the words with the meanings.

1 extinct	3 waste	5 flood
2 laws	4 melt	6 pollution

a official rules that say what people are allowed and not allowed to do ☐
b change from solid to liquid (for example, from ice to water) ☐
c a large amount of water covering an area that is usually dry ☐
d not existing any more ☐
e things that make water, air and the ground unclean ☐
f material that people throw away ☐

6 SPEAKING Work in pairs. Ask and answer questions.

1 Which animals do you know that are extinct or in danger of extinction?
2 What laws to protect the environment are there in your country?
3 What problems with waste are there where you live?
4 What might happen if the ice around the North and South Poles melts?
5 Are floods common in your country?
6 Are the air and water very polluted in your area? What could your class do to help fight pollution?

7 6.02 Match the words in the list with the photos. Write 1–4 in the boxes. Then listen, check and repeat.

A ☐

B ☐

C ☐

D ☐

1 smog | **2** recycling | **3** litter | **4** rubbish

8 Think about the environment in your country. Write notes.

some rivers polluted　*air pollution from factories*

9 SPEAKING Work in pairs. Look at your notes from Exercise 8. Make predictions for the next 30 years. Which environmental issues concern you the most? Then report to the class.

Some of the rivers in our country are polluted, for example … We think this will create big problems for the fish, and …

In some parts of the country, for example in … , the air is polluted. We think this will change. There will be stricter laws so there won't be …

→ workbook page 56

LISTENING

10 Read the headlines in the online newspaper story and look at the images. Write down six words you might find in the article.

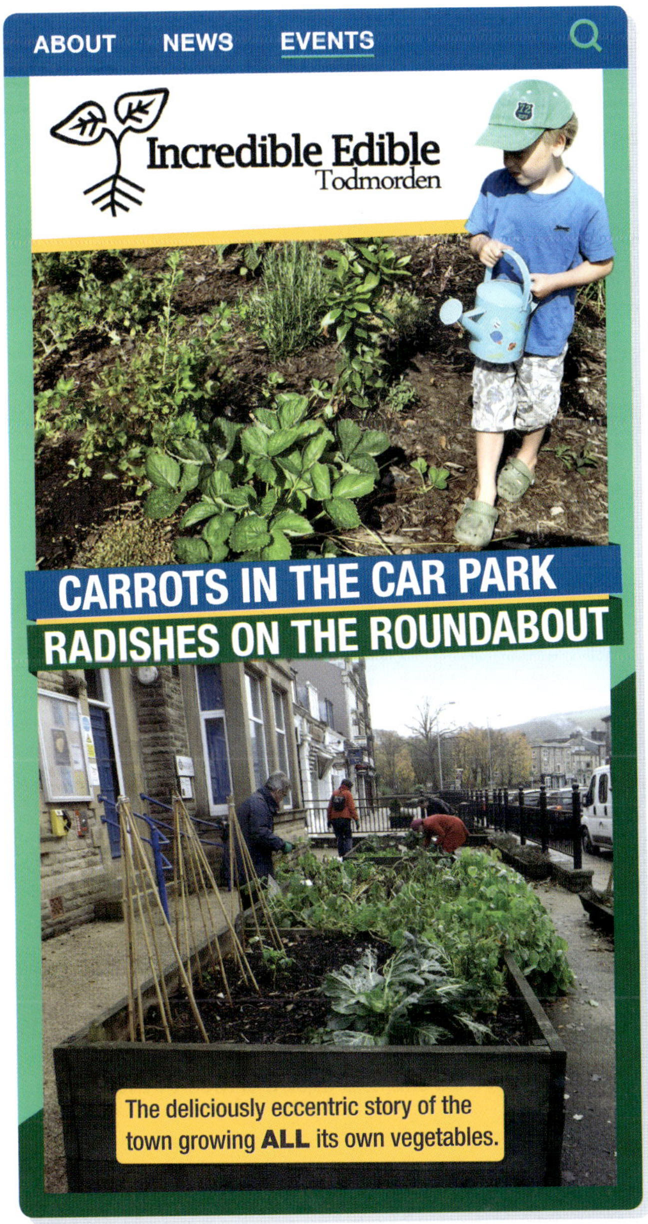

11 6.03 Use the information from the newspaper headlines and your imagination to say what you think is special about the town of Todmorden. Then listen to the story and check your ideas.

12 6.03 Listen again and answer the questions.

1 What's the 'Incredible Edible' project all about?
2 Who takes part in the project?
3 Who had the idea?
4 Why did they decide to do something?
5 What was the reaction to their idea like?

13 Do you think the experiment will last? Why (not)? Would you like to see a similar experiment in your town or neighbourhood?

FUNCTIONS

Expressing surprise and enthusiasm

14 6.03 Listen to the radio programme again. The phrases below can be used to express enthusiasm. Tick (✓) the ones that the reporter uses.

- [ ] Oh, really?
- [ ] Wow!
- [ ] That sounds wonderful!
- [ ] How exciting!
- [ ] That's amazing! (wonderful! etc.)
- [ ] What a brilliant idea!
- [ ] Incredible! (Cool! Fascinating! etc.)

15 Put the dialogue in order. Read it out with a partner.

- [ ] A He's offered me a role in his next film.
- [ ] A I'm only going to meet Steven Spielberg.
- [ ] A I'm going to California this summer.
- [ ] A Three hours.
- [ ] B Cool!
- [ ] B Oh, really? Only three hours. Why's that?
- [ ] B How exciting! What are you going to talk about?
- [ ] B Wow! That sounds exciting. How long are you going to stay there?

16 SPEAKING Practise dialogues with a partner. A says something surprising, B reacts, using one of the expressions from Exercise 14, and asks a question. A says something surprising again, etc. Use your own ideas, or the ones here.

- go to the moon
- meet Zendaya
- win a big prize
- see an alien
- only eat white food
- stay up all night

Train to TH!NK

Different perspectives

1 **Read these different texts. Match them with the text types in the list. Write numbers 1–4. Give your reasons. There are two text types you don't need to use.**

- ☐ note
- ☐ diary entry
- ☐ text message
- ☐ online article
- ☐ informative leaflet
- ☐ adventure story

1
This morning we took part in the Incredible Edible project. I was so proud when I saw that all of the students in my class had brought vegetable plants …

2
Meeting the guys who want to plant vegetables by the football field at 5… Hope to CUL8R. S.

3
… to buy OUR vegetables. They come from local farms. They are organic and fresh – and you don't have to pick them yourself. Prices are reasonable; the quality is high!

4
Our reporter has learned that the council will publish a list of spare land that can be used by the Incredible Edible project. It has been …

2 SPEAKING **Work in pairs. Discuss who the texts are for and what their purpose is.**

I think text 1 is probably for … I think somebody wrote it in order to …

READING

3 6.04 **Read and listen to the text. What type of text is it? Choose from the text types in Exercise 1. Who might this text be for?**

ENERGY MATTERS

Unless we change our behaviour, our planet won't survive. To produce electricity, we burn coal and oil, known as fossil fuels, but creating energy in this way puts CO_2 into the air and causes air pollution and smog. As a result, we are destroying our Earth. What can we do to solve these problems? If we use renewable energy, it will provide us with cleaner air and water. So what is renewable energy? It is energy that doesn't use up the resource used to make it. Solar power, wind power and hydroelectric power are examples of renewable energy sources.

SOLAR POWER

Using the power of the sun produces very little pollution and it is also much cheaper than using fossil fuels. Morocco is now using solar power in a big way. When we say big, we mean big! They have the largest solar plant on Earth. Its wind and hydroelectric power plants will soon provide half of Morocco's electricity. Morocco might become the world's superpower in solar energy, producing enough electricity for one million homes.

HYDROELECTRIC POWER AND WIND FARMS

In the past, Turkey relied on fossil fuels and natural gas to produce electricity. In recent years, it has increased its use of renewable energy. Private companies have built nine small hydroelectric power plants and they use river water stored in dams to produce electricity. They have also built six wind farms, and they have set up 20 other renewable energy projects. Wind power is another clean alternative to fossil fuels. It is everywhere! Wind farms use very little land and they don't use any water.

A SIMPLE WAY TO REDUCE ENERGY

Something simple that everyone could do to help save the environment: using energy-saving light bulbs. Mexico has given almost 23 million of them to families for free. Now, more than 5.5 million Mexican families use energy-saving light bulbs. If they use energy-saving light bulbs, they may save up to 18% on their electricity bill. This is a simple thing that YOU can do, too. You will use a tenth of the electricity if you use energy-saving light bulbs at home.

4 **Work in pairs. Cover up the text and try to complete the sentences.**

1. In order to survive, we will need to …
2. In the past, Turkey relied on …
3. In recent years, Turkey has …
4. Mexico has given away 23 million free …

5 **Read the text again. Which of the ideas …**

- do you think is best?
- has the most direct effect on people's lives?
- would be easy or difficult to do in your country?

GRAMMAR

First conditional; *unless* in first conditional sentences

6 Complete the sentences with the correct form of the verbs. Look at the leaflet on page 60 and check your answers. Then choose the right answers to make the rules.

1 If we use renewable energy, it ______ (provide) us with cleaner air and water.
2 Unless we change our behaviour, our planet ______ (not survive).
3 You ______ (use) a tenth of the electricity if you use energy-saving light bulbs at home.

> **RULE:** We use the first conditional to talk about the consequences of a [4]**possible** / **impossible** future action.
> - Condition clause: ***if*** + present simple
> - Result clause: ***will*** / ***won't*** + main verb
>
> The condition clause can come before or after the result clause.
> *Unless* means [5]**only if** / **if not**.

7 Match the parts of the sentences.

1 Unless someone lends me a bit of money, ☐
2 I'll only be able to go to the concert ☐
3 They won't pass the exam ☐
4 Won't she miss the train ☐

a if my dad drives me there.
b if she doesn't leave for the station now?
c I won't be able to take the bus home.
d unless they study hard.

8 Write first conditional sentences. Then decide in which of them you could use *unless*.

0 environment / suffer / if / we not recycle more
The environment will suffer if we don't recycle more.
The environment will suffer unless we recycle more.
1 if / I give this phone / charity / they find someone who needs it
2 if / this tap not stop dripping / how much water / we waste in a day?
3 situation / become worse / if they not change behaviour
4 Look – battery full! / if you not disconnect charger / you waste energy
5 if she read this book / she understand situation better
6 if / you not stop shouting / I not listen any more

9 Complete the questions. Use the correct form of the verbs.

0 What *will* you *do* if they *don't help* you? (do / not help)
1 If you ________ , ________ you ________ good marks in your test? (not study / get)
2 Unless the weather ________ really bad on Sunday, we ________ to the beach. (be / go)
3 If she ________ you to her birthday party, ________ you ________ her a present? (invite / buy)
4 She ________ him unless he ________ her very nicely. (not help / ask)
5 If I ________ to visit you, ________ you ________ me around your town? (come / show)

10 SPEAKING Work in pairs. Ask and answer questions using the first conditional. Use your own ideas or the ones here.

1 What will you do if it rains all weekend?
2 What will you buy if you get some extra money this month?
3 What will you do tonight if you don't have any homework?

→ workbook page 55

VOCABULARY

Verbs to talk about energy

11 6.05 Match the verbs with their definitions. Write 1–8. Listen and check.

> **1** to reuse | **2** to throw away | **3** to recycle
> **4** to waste | **5** to charge | **6** to disconnect
> **7** to save | **8** to leave on standby

a to not switch an appliance off completely so it is ready to be used at any time ☐
b to collect and treat rubbish in order to produce useful materials that can be used again ☐
c to fill up an empty battery again ☐
d to get rid of something ☐
e to stop something from being wasted ☐
f to stop the connection between an electrical appliance and the power source ☐
g to use something again ☐
h to use too much of something or use it incorrectly ☐

12 SPEAKING Work in pairs. Discuss these questions.

1 Do you waste a lot of energy? What could you do to save energy?
2 What things do you reuse?
3 What things do you recycle? Do you think there is enough recycling done where you live? Why?

→ workbook page 56

TH!NK

Green solutions around the world

Culture

1 Look at the photos. Where do you think these places might be?

2 6.06 Read and listen to the article. Check your ideas.

GREEN SOLUTIONS AROUND THE WORLD

THE NETHERLANDS

Can a ban on cars help business?

In the mid-seventies, there was a problem in the city of Groningen, in the Netherlands. Lots of people used the motorway in the city centre and there were too many cars. This caused a lot of traffic jams. The city council decided to replace the motorway with green areas, pedestrian areas, cycleways and bus lanes. They stopped cars from parking in the market square and discouraged cars from entering the city centre.

At first, shop owners said they would lose customers. But they didn't, and soon businesses and shops which were not in the car-free zone wanted the council to expand it.

Today, 61% of trips taken in the city are done by bicycle. The city centre is full of places for bikes to park and most buildings have bicycle garages. As a result, today Groningen has got the cleanest air of any big Dutch city.

ECUADOR

Can a camera trap programme help save a nature park?

The Bigal River nature park is located between the Amazon forest and the Andes. It is a beautiful area, and is home to many different animals and birds. However, human activity has had a negative effect on the wildlife that lives there. Many animals and birds are endangered because of loss of habitat and hunting.

To show people how wonderful the nature park is, the Sumac Muyu Foundation set up camera traps around the park. These traps record a video whenever an animal enters a certain place in the park. It shows where they are in the park, and it studies changes in behaviour caused by humans.

The camera traps have been in the nature park since 2014. They have collected hundreds of hours of film showing wildlife, and the material is being used to help fight new building projects in the protected land.

MEXICO

Can a wood-burning stove really be environmentally friendly and still be efficient?

People in many countries still rely on open fires. Although the fires help people cook and stay warm, the smoke and gas can cause illnesses. They also use precious fuels such as wood or coal. The so-called Patsari stove uses less wood and so it improves both air quality in the home and family health.

The stove was developed in Mexico. It is made of sealed-together brick stones so no gas can come out from the stove. The stones heat up when somebody lights a fire underneath, and the back of the stove is attached to a chimney, which takes the smoke out of the home.

Health studies show that families with a Patsari stove get 30% fewer lung infections and 50% fewer eye infections.

3 SPEAKING Work in pairs. Read these things people say. Are they from the Netherlands, Mexico or Ecuador?

1 'People in our town feel much healthier now.'
2 'I hope those birds don't disappear.'
3 'I still get a lot of customers in my restaurant.'
4 'We're happy that they didn't build there – and the video certainly helped.'
5 'It's much nicer inside my house now.'
6 'I never have a problem – there's always somewhere to leave it.'

4 Do you know of any other towns, cities or countries where there has been an environmental project?

5 VOCABULARY There are eight highlighted words in the article. Match the words with these meanings. Write the words.

0 an organ in the chest that you use to breathe *lung*
1 the place where an animal or plant usually lives ______
2 things that people or animals do, or the way they act ______
3 of great value because of being rare, expensive or important ______
4 the result of an action or other cause ______
5 tried to prevent something from happening ______
6 very tightly closed ______
7 make something bigger ______

PRONUNCIATION
/f/, /v/, /b/ consonant sounds
Go to page 120.

WRITING
An article for the school magazine

1 INPUT **Read this article from a school magazine. Then answer the questions.**

1 How has the river changed?
2 What are the main reasons for the problems?
3 What will happen if the situation doesn't change?
4 What should be done?

2 **Put the words in the correct order to make sentences from the article. Then go through it and find the evidence the writer uses to support each of these statements.**

1 so / the / beautiful / once / Quiller River / was
2 situation / alarming / is / the
3 the / riverbanks / and / look at / just

3 **Match the sentence halves. Which of them talk about possible consequences? Which are suggestions? Which are predictions?**

1 If politicians wake up and we all do something, ☐
2 We need stricter laws ☐
3 In a few years' time ☐
4 So I really think politicians ☐
5 The situation will be even worse in a few years ☐

a to protect our river.
b unless factories stop polluting the water.
c we might once again be able to enjoy the beauty of the river.
d should do something about it.
e all the fish may be dead.

4 ANALYSE **The article has four paragraphs. Which of them …**

a expresses the writer's hope that the situation will be better in the future?
b introduces the topic?
c describes problems and says what should be done?
d describes problems, says what will happen if nothing is done and what should be done?

Quiller River POLLUTION

The Quiller River was once so beautiful that there is even a song about it. And now?

The situation is alarming. There are lots of factories along the river. Newspapers have recently reported that the water in the river is totally polluted. There are hardly any fish left, and the water itself smells terrible. The situation will be even worse in a few years unless factories stop polluting the water. That is why I really think politicians should do something about it. We need stricter laws to protect our river.

And just look at the riverbanks. They are covered in litter. It seems that there are lots of people who throw their waste into the river. This must stop! We should all get together and help clean up the riverbanks.

In conclusion, if politicians wake up and we all do something, we might once again be able to enjoy the beauty of the river. Let's hope it's not too late.

5 PLAN **Choose a local environmental problem and make notes about what the situation is now, possible consequences and what should be done.**

6 PRODUCE **Write an article for your school magazine raising awareness about the environmental issue you have chosen.**

- Find a good title.
- Write an introduction that catches the reader's interest.
- Describe what the problems are, what you think the consequences might be and what should be done.

B1 Preliminary for Schools

READING

Part 5: 4-option multiple-choice cloze

→ workbook page 79

1 **For each question, choose the correct answer.**

GLOBAL fishing crisis

A growing concern around the world is how the food production industry is being affected by changes in the environment. For example, millions of people around the world consider fish to be an important part of their [1]______ diet. However, fishing to meet this demand has become a major environmental issue, along with animal extinction, air [2]______ and global warming.

Certain [3]______ of fish are in danger and are no longer found in their usual feeding areas, so fishing boats must travel further out to sea to catch fish. More fishermen are now choosing to catch rarer fish to sell at higher prices, which is affecting populations of less [4]______ fish.

Unfortunately, the problem of overfishing is getting worse and some fish populations could possibly [5]______ out if certain changes aren't put in place. Many people know that we need to [6]______ our oceans and sea life, so they are fighting for stricter fishing laws.

	A	B	C	D
1	regular	frequent	proper	ordinary
2	climate	pollution	condition	damage
3	collections	numbers	descriptions	species
4	ordinary	common	usual	typical
5	blow	carry	run	wear
6	protect	care	prevent	keep

LISTENING

Part 2: 3-option multiple choice

→ workbook page 35

2 6.09 **Listen to six short conversations. For each question, choose the correct answer.**

1 You will hear a girl and her brother talking about the girl's night with her two friends.
What does the girl say about the night out?
- **A** Everyone thought the film was incredibly funny.
- **B** The most enjoyable part of her night took place after the film.
- **C** She learned some surprising information about school from her friends.

2 Listen to a man and a woman talking about a tennis match.
What does the man say about the match?
- **A** He disagrees with the coach's decision.
- **B** He thinks the match wasn't very exciting.
- **C** He doesn't understand the actions of the coach.

3 Listen to a boy and a girl talking about the boy's phone.
What does the boy say about the phone?
- **A** Every time he has a conversation, the phone switches off.
- **B** When the battery is running out, the phone always switches off.
- **C** There are two things wrong with the phone.

4 You will hear a boy and a woman in a shop.
Why does the boy want to change the pullover?
- **A** It's the wrong size and the wrong colour.
- **B** It was too expensive.
- **C** He would rather have a T-shirt.

5 Listen to two friends talking.
What has the girl done?
- **A** She has changed the colour of her hair.
- **B** She has had her hair cut and changed the colour.
- **C** She has had her hair cut shorter than it was before.

6 Listen to two friends talking about music at a party.
What did the girl think about the music?
- **A** She didn't enjoy listening to the band.
- **B** She wanted to dance, but the music wasn't great.
- **C** The DJ didn't play good music for dancing.

TEST YOURSELF UNITS 5 & 6

VOCABULARY

1 Complete the sentences with the words in the list. There are two extra words.

charge | enter | extinct | flood | melt | record | release
standby | stream | throw away | tour | waste

1 Is it OK if I ______________________ my mobile phone in your room?
2 It's getting warm now, so I think the snow will ______________________ soon.
3 Don't ______________________ water. You shouldn't stay in the shower for more than four minutes!
4 It's really easy to ______________________ songs – all you need is an internet connection!
5 They've made a new record, and they're going to ______________________ it next week.
6 You can't win the competition if you don't ______________________ it!
7 After the band released their new record, they went on ______________________ for six months.
8 If it carries on raining like this, there might be a ______________________ tonight.
9 There aren't many of these monkeys left in the world. They could be ______________________ in a few years.
10 Don't switch it off completely – leave it on ______________________ , OK?

/10

GRAMMAR

2 Complete the sentences with the words in the list.

have been playing | have played | if | might not | unless | won't

1 I didn't study for the test. I ______________________ pass it, I'm sure!
2 Sorry, Mum. My shirt is really dirty. I ______________________ football in the park.
3 We won't have a picnic ______________________ it rains.
4 I don't feel very well, so I ______________________ go to the cinema tonight. I'm not sure.
5 I'll never finish this washing up ______________________ you help me. Please!
6 Everyone in the team is really tired. We ______________________ three games this week already!

3 Find and correct the mistake in each sentence.

1 He's being working here for over five months.
2 If it will rain, we'll stay at home.
3 I've been writing forty invitations for the party next week.
4 We might to go to the game later.
5 You won't do well in the test unless you don't study.
6 Ouch! I've been cutting my hand.

/12

FUNCTIONAL LANGUAGE

4 Complete the mini-dialogues with the words in the list.

bit | feeling | how | matter | news | not | sounds | up

1 A Hi, Paul. What's the ______________________ ?
B Nothing much. I'm just a ______________________ upset.
2 A What's ______________________ , Olivia? Why are you crying?
B I'm crying because I'm happy. I won a competition.
A ______________________ exciting! I'm really happy for you.
3 A How are you ______________________ ?
B Well, ______________________ great. But I'll be OK, I think.
4 A I've got some ______________________ . We're going to get a new dog.
B That ______________________ great! I'm sure you're really happy.

/8

MY SCORE /30

22–30 | 10–21 | 0–9

7 THE FUTURE IS NOW

OBJECTIVES

FUNCTIONS: checking information; agreeing

GRAMMAR: future forms; question tags; *nor, neither* and *so*

VOCABULARY: future time expressions; arranging a party; phrases with *about*

Get THINKING

Watch the video and think:
how will the world be different 50 years from now?

READING

1 **Look at the photo. What can you see? Discuss your ideas.**

2 **Look at the pictures in the newspaper on the next page. What do they show?**

This one shows a spacecraft travelling to another planet.

3 SPEAKING **Work in pairs. Talk about a news story for each of the following newspaper sections.**

communication | food | science | travel

Can you think of a science story?

Yes, machines to automatically clean everything inside your house.

4 **Read the stories on the next page quickly. What is 'different' about this newspaper?**

5 7.01 **Read and listen to the stories again. Mark the sentences T (true) or F (false).**

1 It will take SS Marstrek more than one Earth day to get to Mars. ____
2 There will only be two passengers on the first SS Marstrek flight. ____
3 The meeting about meat production started last Monday. ____
4 Two groups of people will celebrate outside the building. ____
5 By 2050, people will only need 60 minutes' rest a day. ____
6 A journalist will be the first person to test the new device. ____
7 To send a thought message, you need a handheld device. ____
8 Dr Andrea Gomez says it will always be necessary to have a device for thought messaging. ____

6 SPEAKING **Work with a partner. Correct the false sentences in Exercise 5.**

TODAY'S WORLD

22nd July 2042

TRAVEL

FASTER TO MARS

Tomorrow will be another great day in the history of space flight when the SS Marstrek makes its first journey to Mars. The spaceship will carry passengers to the red planet in just 28 hours – three days faster than any other passenger flight! The spacecraft takes off at 10 o'clock in the morning and arrives the next day at 3 o'clock in the afternoon (Mars time). Among the passengers on this exciting first flight will be singer Marion Hyde and actor Karl Costly. To begin with, there will only be one flight a week. But with tickets costing $500,000 each, few of us will be flying on the SS Marstrek just yet!

FOOD

WILL MEAT BE HISTORY SOON?

Government ministers from over 50 countries are meeting on Monday next week to discuss stopping all meat production in their countries. One minister who will be at the meeting said yesterday, 'We know how much people like eating meat. But the fact is that more and more people are becoming vegetarian. We also know that meat production is very bad for the environment. And, of course, we should think about the animals themselves.'

There will be a lot of demonstrators outside the building where the meeting is held. Animal rights groups say they are going there to celebrate, while many cattle farmers also plan to be there, to ask the ministers to think again about the plans.

SCIENCE

SLEEP TO BECOME 'A THING OF THE PAST'

Sleep will become unnecessary by 2050, say scientists. They are working on a device which will make sleep a thing of the past. Instead of going to bed, all a person will have to do is put their hands up against a charger and rest for about half an hour. After that, they will not feel tired any more. Doing this once a day will be enough for most people to stay awake for 24 hours. They are going to start tests next month to make sure that there are no negative side effects. The first human to test the device will be journalist Glenn Martin.

COMMUNICATION

SENDING MESSAGES BY THINKING

Thought messaging! Imagine that you want to send a message to your friend.

So, instead of writing a message, all you do is pick up your handheld device, think 'message Jim' and then you think the content of your message ('Hi Jim, how about coffee tomorrow morning?'). The message goes automatically to your handheld device, which writes it and sends it to Jim!

At a conference yesterday, Dr Andrea Gomez, Chief Scientist at the Steiger Institute, told the audience that this will be possible in two years' time, but she stressed that it will never be possible to send thoughts directly from one person to another without a device.

TH!NK values

Believe in a better future

7 **What kind of future do you think these stories show?**

- 😀 a positive future
- 😐 not positive or negative
- ☹ a negative future

- ◯ Travel to Mars
- ◯ No more meat
- ◯ No more sleep
- ◯ Thought messages

8 SPEAKING **Work in pairs. Compare your ideas with your partner. Give reasons.**

I think the story about stopping meat production shows a positive future because then animals won't be killed any more.

9 SPEAKING **Think of a positive future. What will it be like? Think about these things.**

medicine | poverty | sport
technology | weather | world peace

No one is hungry.

GRAMMAR
Future forms

1 Complete the example sentences with the verbs in the list. Check your answers with the stories on page 67. Then match the sentences with the rules. Write a–d.

meeting | start | takes | will

a The spacecraft ______ off at 10 o'clock in the morning.
b Government ministers from over 50 countries are ______ on Monday next week.
c Sleep ______ become unnecessary by 2050.
d They are going to ______ tests next month.

RULE: We often use
- the present simple tense to talk about fixed future events. [1]______
- *be going to* to talk about future plans and intentions. [2]______
- *will/won't* to make predictions about the future. [3]______
- the present continuous to talk about future arrangements. [4]______

2 Complete the sentences. Use the present simple form of the verbs in the list.

arrive | ~~finish~~ | leave | open | start

0 The sale *finishes on Friday* ______.
1 The shop ______.
2 Flight FL098 ______.
3 The concert ______.
4 The train ______.

3 Read the sentences. Mark them P (prediction), I (intention), A (arrangement) or F (fixed event).

1 She won't do very well in her exams. ______
2 They're going to buy a new car soon. ______
3 The match starts at 3 pm. ______
4 He's meeting his mother for lunch on Friday. ______
5 The new zoo opens on Friday. ______
6 One day we'll all live under the sea. ______
7 I'm going to write a novel one day. ______
8 They're having a party on Tuesday. ______

4 Choose the best future form to complete the dialogue.

A [0]*Are you doing* / *Do you do* anything on Friday evening?
B Yes, I [1]*'m working* / *'ll work* at the restaurant.
A Oh, what time [2]*are you finishing* / *do you finish*?
B The restaurant usually closes at 9 pm and I work until then, but there's a party this Friday so I [3]*won't* / *don't* finish until at least 10 pm. Why?
A Well, I [4]*'m having* / *'ll have* a party. Lots of people [5]*come* / *are coming* and I wanted to invite you, too.
B I'd love to come.
A You [6]*won't be* / *aren't being* too tired?
B No way. It [7]*is being* / *will be* the perfect way to start the weekend.

→ workbook page 64

VOCABULARY
Future time expressions

5 Complete the time expressions with the words in the list.

after | from | later | long | near | next (x2) | time

1 the week after ______
2 before too ______
3 in two weeks' ______
4 ______ weekend
5 the day ______ tomorrow
6 ______ today
7 four years ______ now
8 in the ______ future

6 Complete these sentences with your own ideas. Think about your family, friends, school, town and country.

Predictions
1 I think ______ in the near future.
2 I think ______ 40 years from now.
3 I think ______ in 20 years' time.

Intentions
4 I ______ the week after next.
5 I ______ next Friday.
6 I ______ before too long.

Arrangements
7 I ______ this weekend.
8 I ______ later today.
9 I ______ tomorrow morning.

→ workbook page 66

LISTENING

7 **You are going to listen to two interviews with people from the news stories on page 67: singer Marion Hyde and journalist Glenn Martin. Work in pairs. Write three questions to ask Marion or Glenn.**

- Student A: Write three questions to ask Marion.
- Student B: Write three questions to ask Glenn.

8 SPEAKING **Compare your questions with your partner.**

9 7.02 **Listen to the interviews. Do they ask your questions? What questions do they ask?**

10 7.02 **Listen again. Choose the correct answer A, B or C.**

1 What is one of Marion's plans for her time on Mars?

2 What else might she do?

3 What is Glenn going to take with him when he does the tests?

4 What kind of work is he going to do?

WordWise: Phrases with *about*

11 **Complete the sentences from the unit so far with a phrase from the list.**

sorry about | about half an hour | how about | think about | about to

1 We should ______________________ the animals themselves.
2 All a person will have to do is put their hands up against a charger and rest for ______________________ .
3 Hi Jim, ______________________ coffee tomorrow morning?
4 We're talking to Marion Hyde as she's ______________________ board the SS Marstrek.
5 Oh dear! ______________________ that! You won't get bored?

12 **Match the questions and answers.**

1 How tall is Jack? ☐
2 You haven't tidied up! ☐
3 I'm tired. How about a rest? ☐
4 Has your sister left school now? ☐
5 John had an accident yesterday. ☐

a Yes. She's about to go to university.
b About 1 metre 65, I think.
c Yes, I heard about it. Is he OK?
d Yes, OK.
e Oh, sorry about that.

13 SPEAKING **Complete these sentences so they are true for you. Then compare with a partner.**

1 I usually get up at about …
2 When I think about the future, I …
3 I've got a friend who is about to …

→ workbook page 66

READING

1 **Imagine you are organising a party. Put these things in order of importance.**

- ☐ food
- ☐ music
- ☐ venue (where you are going to have the party)
- ☐ decorations
- ☐ invitations

2 SPEAKING **Work in pairs. Compare your answers to Exercise 1.**

A special venue's not very important. I'll just use my house.

Music's very important. You can't have a party without good music.

3 **Read the messages quickly. What kind of party are they arranging? Do you think Becky is a good organiser?**

4 7.03 **Read and listen to the messages again. Who is responsible for each of the things in Exercise 1?**

Messages

Becky: Hi everyone. Just want to check some things for the big surprise party next week.

Mark: Hey everyone! I'm looking forward to the party!!

Joanna: So am I. Anyone heard from Simon? He's never around, is he?

Mark: He'll reply later, I'm sure. But good news – he's hired the hall for the party.

Becky: Well, that is good news, isn't it? By the way, you haven't said anything to Paula, have you?

Joanna: No, I haven't said anything.

Mark: Nor have I. I'm not a fool, Becky.

Becky: Sorry. I'm just a bit anxious, that's all. It's not easy to keep something a secret when you have to talk to about 30 people about it! By the way, I've sent out the invitations.

Simon: Hi guys, just reading messages now! No signal on the train – sorry about that. I didn't miss anything important, did I?

Mark: No, not really.

Becky: Now, is the food organised? Simon?

Simon: Yes, my parents are going to make pizzas. We've got permission to be there from 4 pm. That should be OK, shouldn't it?

Joanna: Yes! My mum and I are making desserts. It's all taken care of.

Becky: Brilliant. What about decorations, Mark?

Mark: That's not me, that's you, Becky.

Becky: Are you sure? How could I have forgotten?

Mark: Didn't you write it down?

Becky: Yes. I always write things down. But then I forgot to look at my notes!

Simon: Don't worry, I can help decorate the hall.

Joanna: So can I. Quick question, how are we going to get Paula to go to the hall on the day? We need a plan, don't we?

Becky: Argh! I haven't thought about that yet.

Simon: Neither have we. Don't worry, Becky, you can't do everything.

Mark: Here's an idea. I'll say I'm taking her to the cinema and we'll stop at the hall on the way.

Joanna: She isn't going to believe that, is she? We need a better idea than that.

Simon: Just thought of something else – what about the music? Has anyone booked a DJ?

Becky: Oh, no!

GRAMMAR
Question tags

5 Complete the sentences. Look at the messages on page 70 and check your answers.

1 He's never around, ______ he?
2 You haven't said anything to Paula, ______ you?
3 I didn't miss anything important, ______ I?
4 That should be OK, ______ it?
5 We need a plan, ______ we?
6 She isn't going to believe that, ______ she?

6 Use the sentences in Exercise 5 to complete the rules.

RULE: Question tags are short questions which we use to check facts or make conversation.
- With positive statements, use a [0]*negative* question tag.
- With negative statements, use a [1]________ question tag. (sentence 2)
- When *be* is used in the statement, repeat it in the question tag. (sentences 1, 6)
- With present or past simple verbs, use [2]________, *don't, does*, [3]________ (present simple) or [4]________, *didn't* (past simple). (sentences 3, 5)
- With modal verbs (*can, might*, etc.) and most other verb forms, repeat the modal or the auxiliary verb in the question tag. (sentence 4)

7 Complete the questions with tags.

0 She sings beautifully, *doesn't she* ?
1 You won't say anything, ________________ ?
2 Claudia didn't phone, ________________ ?
3 You can come to my party, ________________ ?
4 He's Jamie's brother, ________________ ?
5 That meal was delicious, ________________ ?
6 They don't live with you, ________________ ?
7 You've met Leon, ________________ ?
8 You aren't going to university, ________________ ?

Nor, neither and *so*

8 Complete the sentences. Then complete the rules.

Mark I'm looking forward to the party.
Joanna So [1]______ I.
Simon I can help with the decorations.
Joanna So [2]______ I.
Joanna No, I haven't said anything.
Mark Nor [3]______ I.
Becky I haven't thought about that yet.
Simon Neither [4]______ we.

RULE: We can use *so* and *nor/neither* to agree with statements.
- We use [5]______ to agree with positive statements.
- We use [6]______ to agree with negative statements.

After *so* and *nor/neither* we repeat the verb used in the statement. If the statement is in the present or past simple, we use *do/did* to agree with it. (See rules on question tags.)

9 Write replies to agree with the statements.

0 I love school. *So do I.*
1 I didn't watch any TV last night. ________________
2 I can't go to the party. ________________
3 I should do my homework. ________________
4 I'm going to bed early tonight. ________________
5 I don't eat meat. ________________
6 I won't be late. ________________
7 I was very upset with Tim. ________________

→ workbook page 65

PRONUNCIATION
Intonation of question tags Go to page 121.

VOCABULARY
Arranging a party

10 Match the verbs with the nouns to create a 'to do' list. Use the posts on page 70 to help you. Use one of the nouns twice.

Verbs
book | decorate
get | hire | organise
send out

Nouns
DJ | food and drinks
invitations | permission
room

Get permission for the party.

11 SPEAKING Work in pairs. In what order should you do the things on your to do list?

You should get permission first, shouldn't you?

→ workbook page 66

WRITING
An invitation to a party

12 You are having a party. Write the invitations. Be sure to mention the date, time and place of the party and also what your guests should bring (or not bring).

DEVELOPING SPEAKING

1 7.06 **Look at the photos. It's Friday evening. What do you think they are talking about? Listen and read to check.**

Hannah: So, Friday evening, it's finally the weekend. Thank goodness! I've had a really hard week.

Tracey: So have I. There's nothing wrong with Mr Gordon but he gives so much homework! I've never had so much work to do in my life! But next week we've got two days off at my school!

Hannah: Lucky you! But listen, let's do something together at the weekend.

Tracey: Yes, let's. Got any ideas about what we could do?

Hannah: How about a picnic? I haven't had a picnic … well, in a long time!

Tracey: Neither have I. That's a great idea. But the weather forecast isn't good for Saturday, and I'm busy on Sunday morning …

Hannah: Oh, that's a shame. Well, what about Sunday afternoon? What do you reckon?

Tracey: Sunday afternoon sounds fine. Let's hope the weather's nice. Picnics are always better on sunny days. Oh! Hang on! On Sunday afternoon I'm taking my gran out. Mum and Dad usually take her somewhere, but it's my turn this Sunday.

Hannah: Can't you take her out in the morning?

Tracey: Not really. We always take her out in the afternoon. It's important for her to have a routine – I don't want to change that.

Hannah: OK, ask your brother to take her.

Tracey: Well, he's got football and, anyway, he took her out last week. Sorry.

Hannah: In other words, we can't have our picnic. I was looking forward to it!

Tracey: So was I, Hannah. I'd love to have a picnic, but, you know. I hope we can do it next weekend.

Hannah: So do I. I'll call you. And I'll try to be a bit more flexible than you. Bye, Tracey!

Tracey: Oh Hannah, don't be …

2 **Read the dialogue again and answer the questions.**

1 Why was last week hard for Tracey?
2 What does Hannah suggest they do this weekend?
3 Why can't they do it on Saturday?
4 What is Tracey doing on Sunday afternoon?

3 SPEAKING **Discuss the statements in pairs. What do you think?**

1 Tracey could talk to her grandmother and change her plans.
2 Tracey isn't very flexible.
3 Hannah could be more understanding.

Phrases for fluency

4 **Find the underlined expressions in the dialogue and use them to complete the conversations.**

1 A My parents just won a holiday in a competition.
B Wow! [1]___________!
A The holiday is for two people, so I can't go.
B Oh, [2]___________.

2 A How's Ben? Any news?
B Yes. He's OK. His arm's not broken. [3]___________.
A [4]___________, it's not as serious as we thought.

3 A Look at that guy's clothes. They're horrible! [5]___________?
B Well, I don't like them much. But I don't think you should be so critical.
A Hey! [6]___________ saying what you think!

FUNCTIONS
Agreeing

KEY LANGUAGE

a So do I.	**c** Neither have I.
b So have I.	**d** So was I.

5 **Match the sentences to the replies in the Key Language box.**

1 I've had a really hard week. ☐
2 I haven't had a picnic for a long time. ☐
3 I was looking forward to it. ☐
4 I hope we can do it next weekend. ☐

6 SPEAKING **Complete these sentences with true information about you. Then find people who agree with you and write their names.**

Tonight I'm going to ___________
and so is ___________.
I'm not going to ___________
nor is ___________.
Yesterday I ___________
and so did ___________.
Yesterday I didn't ___________
nor did ___________.

LIFE COMPETENCIES

Being flexible means being willing to change your plans or ideas if a situation changes. We can't always do what we want, often because friends or family have different ideas or plans. But sometimes, being flexible helps to create a positive result.

1 ▶ 21 Watch the video. What did Kieran want to talk about and why couldn't he?

2 ▶ 21 Watch again and answer the questions.

1 Why do buildings need to be flexible?
2 Why did Kieran want to eat earlier one Saturday?
3 Why did his mother say no to his request one day?
4 What did Kieran think about her decision?

3 Read the phone conversation. What does Jade want to do?

Jade I've just bought Urban Quest!
Nicole Wow! I've heard it's amazing.
Jade Me, too. So I thought that maybe ...
Nicole Sorry, I can't. I'm going to see Steve.
Jade Come on! This is Urban Quest!
Nicole No, he's been really bored since he broke his leg playing basketball. I promised I'd go and see him.
Jade Nicole, listen. I've been excited about this for weeks and weeks. You, me, the big TV in the living room and the best computer game of the year.
Nicole Really sorry, Jade. I promised.
Jade Mum said we can order pizzas if you come.
Nicole I'd like to, but I can't. Why don't you come to Steve's, too? I'm sure we can play it there.
Jade But Steve's a terrible player! It'll be boring. And he doesn't have a big TV. Please! I'm going crazy! Playing alone isn't as much fun.
Nicole I know, but why don't you come anyway? We can play at your house next weekend.
Jade I don't know ...

4 SPEAKING Work in pairs. Discuss these questions with your partner.

1 How does Jade feel?
2 How do you think Jade will feel if she stays at home?
3 How do you think Nicole feels after speaking with Jade?
4 What do you think will happen if Jade goes to Steve's house?
5 What should Jade and Nicole do?

Me and my world

5 SPEAKING Work in pairs. What would you do in these situations?

1 It's Saturday morning and you want to go shopping for trainers. Your friend wants to come, too, but he's busy. He's free this afternoon.
2 Your friend wants to start a band. You've always wanted to be a singer, but your friend has already asked somebody else. She has asked you to play the drums.
3 You spend a long time writing a story for homework. Your teacher says that it's very good, but then suggests changing the ending.
4 You want to celebrate your birthday at the new pizza place in town. When you call to book a table, they tell you that it's full on that day. They offer you a table for the weekend after.

6 SPEAKING Work in pairs. Talk about a situation in which you had to be flexible.

TIPS FOR BEING FLEXIBLE

- If you're not sure what to do, ask for some time to think before making a decision.
- How will you feel if you aren't flexible? Being inflexible can leave us feeling sad, lonely and angry.
- Don't cause an argument. If you or your family and friends want to do something else, that's OK.

8 SCIENCE AND US

Get THINKING

Watch the video and think: what scientific discoveries are you grateful for?

OBJECTIVES

FUNCTIONS: talking about past habits; talking about imaginary situations; talking about scientific discoveries

GRAMMAR: past simple vs. past continuous (review); *used to*; second conditional; *I wish*

VOCABULARY: direction and movement; science

1

2

3
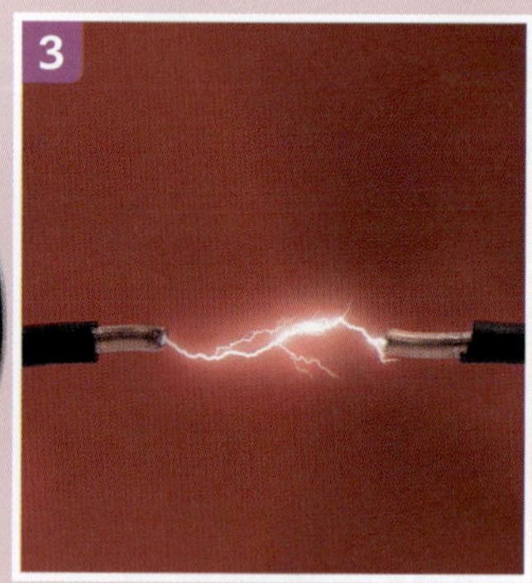

4

5

6

7

READING

1 **Look at the photos. Say what each one shows.**

Picture 3 is electricity.

2 SPEAKING **Work in pairs. Answer the questions.**

1 Why are the things in the photos important?
2 What was life like for people before they had these things?

Before people had fire, they couldn't cook meat. And they were cold in winter.

3 SPEAKING **Work in pairs or small groups. Discuss the questions.**

1 Electricity and fire are *discoveries*. The other things are *inventions*. What's the difference?
2 Which of the things in the photos do you think is the most important? Why?
3 Can you think of other discoveries or inventions that changed how people live?

4 **Look at the pictures on the next page. What do you think the connection between them is?**

5 8.01 **Read and listen to the article. Check your ideas about the pictures.**

6 **Read the article again and answer the questions.**

1 What did Watt notice while he watched the kettle?
2 What did he discover?
3 How did observing the milkmaids influence Jenner's ideas?
4 Why was James Phipps brave?
5 How did Jenner's discovery change the world?

Curious minds

What makes a great scientist? Maybe it's hard work or an interest in understanding how the world works? Yes, these things are important. But one thing that many scientists have in common is that they like to observe – watch – the world carefully. Whether it was Newton watching the apple fall from the tree, or Archimedes watching the water spill out from his bath, scientists like to watch things happen and then start thinking 'why?' Then they investigate a little bit more and what they discover tells us more about the world we live in. Two of the 18th century's greatest discoveries started in exactly this way.

One day in 1748, 12-year-old **James Watt** was sitting in the kitchen, when his aunt started to heat water in a kettle. He was watching the kettle boil, when the lid began to jump up and down. He was curious about it and decided to experiment. He held the lid of the kettle down and noticed that the steam came out of the spout. When he took his hand away, the lid started moving again. James realised that the steam had great power. It was an experiment he never forgot, and years later, he used the ideas to improve the design of the first steam engine.

Another scientist whose observations changed the world was **Edward Jenner**. Back in the late 1700s, there was a terrible disease called smallpox. It killed many people and left many others with horrible injuries. It was an awful disease and there was no cure.

Jenner wanted to do something to help fight the disease. One day he was watching some women working on a farm. The women were getting milk from the cows. While he was watching the women, Jenner had an idea. He knew that fewer people caught smallpox in the countryside than in the city. He also knew that people who worked with cows often caught a disease called cowpox. Cowpox was a less serious disease than smallpox. It made people ill, but didn't kill anybody.

Jenner started to wonder if getting cowpox stopped people from getting smallpox. He decided to test his ideas with the help of a very brave boy called James Phipps. He took some cowpox disease and gave it to James. James caught cowpox and was ill, but got better soon afterwards. Then, Jenner gave James smallpox. Thankfully, James never developed the disease. Jenner's discovery was very important for two reasons. First, because Jenner discovered a way of stopping the spread of smallpox, and second, because he created the world's first vaccine.

Since Jenner's discovery, vaccines have been used around the world and have saved millions of lives.

TH!NK values

How science helps people

7 **Choose the sentence that you think best summarises what the article is about.**

1 Careful observations can lead to great discoveries.
2 You shouldn't believe everything you read about science.
3 Scientists should be more famous than they are.
4 It's important to know something about science.

8 SPEAKING **Compare your ideas with others in the class.**

9 SPEAKING **Here are four things that we have, thanks to science. Write down some more. In pairs, discuss how these things help us every day.**

the internet the telephone medicine the fridge

______________ ______________

______________ ______________

GRAMMAR

Past simple vs. past continuous (review)

1 Complete the sentences from the text on page 75 with the verbs in the correct form. Then complete the rules with *past simple*, *past continuous*, *when* and *while*.

watch x 2 | have | begin

1 He ______ the kettle boil, when the lid ______ to jump up and down.

2 While he ______ the women, Jenner ______ an idea.

> **RULE:** We use
> - the [3]______ for an action that happened at a particular moment in the past. We often use [4]______ with this tense.
> - the [5]______ for a background action or to describe a situation over a period of time in the past. We often use [6]______ with this tense.
>
> Remember that some verbs can't be used in the continuous form.

2 Complete the sentences with the correct past tense form of the verbs.

0 While Benjamin Franklin ___*was watching*___ a thunderstorm, he ___*got*___ some ideas about electricity. (watch / get)

1 We ____________ an experiment at school when a fire ____________. (do / start)

2 They ____________ for lunch because they ____________ enough time. (not stop / not have)

3 The electricity ____________ off at home while I ____________ my homework. (go / do)

4 I ____________ a great science site while I ____________ the net. (discover / surf)

5 Who ____________ you ____________ to when I ____________ you in town yesterday? (talk / see)

6 When the scientist ____________ the answer to the problem, she ____________ very famous. (find / become)

3 Sally saw an incident in her town centre. Complete her statement to the police with the past simple or past continuous form of the verbs in the list. Sometimes more than one verb is possible.

~~buy~~ | cycle | do | go | hit | knock | not stop | ride | ~~sit~~ | see | stand | walk

Last Saturday morning I [0]*bought* a magazine, and I [0]*sat* down on a bench in the town centre to read it. People [1]______ around and [2]______ their shopping. There was a group of four people near me – they [3]______ together and laughing. Then I [4]______ a boy, about 16 years old. He [5]______ his bike down the street. He [6]______ very fast. Suddenly, he had to change direction because there was an old lady in front of him, and he [7]______ right into the group of people. His bike [8]______ a man and [9]______ him over. And the boy [10]______. He just cycled away!

→ workbook page 72

VOCABULARY

Direction and movement

4 Complete the sentence. Then check your answer in the text on page 75.

The lid began to jump ______ and ______.

5 Match the phrases with the pictures.

1 It's coming **towards** her.
2 It's running **away from** her.
3 They're running **around** the tree.
4 She's leaning **backwards**.
5 She's leaning **forwards**.
6 He's walking **up and down** the room.

> **Look**
>
> *Forwards* and *backwards* are the only words here that are never followed by an object.
>
> The words *towards* and *away from* always have an object after them.

6 Which way(s) can these things move?

1 a car
2 a plane
3 a helicopter
4 a lion in a cage

→ workbook page 74

LISTENING

7 Look at the pictures. What ancient beliefs about the world do they show?

8 🔊 8.02 Listen to the science lesson and check your ideas. What other idea do they talk about?

9 🔊 8.02 Listen again. Answer the questions.

1 What can science help us understand?
2 What belief did Copernicus, Galileo and Kepler change?
3 How did Christopher Columbus prove the Earth isn't flat?
4 What did alchemists believe?
5 Why did they think this was possible?
6 What does Mrs Roberts think about the future?

GRAMMAR
used to

10 Complete these sentences with the words in the list. Then choose the correct words to complete the rules.

be | believe | have | think

1 Many people used to ______ that our planet was the centre of the universe.
2 Did people use to______ that the Earth was flat, too?
3 Sailors used to ______ afraid of sailing out too far into the sea.
4 People didn't use to ______ all the scientific equipment we have these days.

RULE: We can use ***used to*** + verb to talk about things that happened regularly in the past but not any more.
In the positive, we say [5]**used to** / **use to** + verb.
In the negative, we say ***didn't*** [6]**used to** / **use to** + verb.
For questions, we say ***Did*** [***you***] [7]**used to** / **use to** + verb.

11 Complete the sentences. Use the correct form of *used to* and the present simple.

0 That shop ___*used to be*___ (be) a book shop, but now it ___*sells*___ (sell) clothes.
1 He ________________ (be) my friend, but we ________________ (not live) near each other any more.
2 When we were younger, we ________________ (not listen) to country music, but now we ________________ (not listen) to anything else.
3 I really ________________ (not like) pizza now, but it ________________ (be) my favourite food.
4 We ________________ (go) to Greece on holiday, but now we ________________ (prefer) Spain.
5 My sister ________________ (believe) there were monsters under her bed.
6 I ________________ (not care) about science, but now I ________________ (think) it's really interesting.
7 When you were small, ________________ you ________________ (have) an imaginary friend?

→ workbook page 72

PRONUNCIATION
The /juː/ sound Go to page 121.

FUNCTIONS
Talking about past habits

12 Think about life when you were little. Write some things that you or others used to do or believe.

____
____
____
____

13 SPEAKING Work in small groups. Talk about the things you wrote. Who has the funniest story?

When I was little I used to think that there was a person inside the post box who took the letters.

My brother and I used to hide in my sister's wardrobe and then jump out and scare her when she opened the door.

READING

1 SPEAKING What would you like to invent? Why? Compare your ideas with a partner.

I'd like to have a flying skateboard.

2 A web forum asked readers what invention would make their life better. Look at the pictures. What things do you think the forum readers suggested?

3 Read the forum. Check your answers to Exercise 2. What other idea is there?

4 8.05 Read and listen to the forum again. Then write the names of the people described in these statements.

1 This person needs more rest. ______
2 This person wants to improve life for everyone. ______
3 This person wants to avoid doing the unpleasant things in life. ______
4 This person wants to go places. ______

Train to TH!NK

Using criteria

5 Here are the four ideas from the forum. Put them in order 1–4 (1 = the most useful, 4 = the least useful).

☐ **a** a clone of yourself
☐ **b** a treatment for tiredness
☐ **c** a super-quick travel machine
☐ **d** a secret laboratory

6 SPEAKING Compare your ideas with a partner.

7 In Exercise 5, you evaluated the ideas on how useful they were. Below are two different criteria. Think of two others.

- How *possible* is it?
- How *important* is it?
- How ______ is it?
- How ______ is it?

8 SPEAKING Choose one of the criteria in Exercise 7 and order the things in Exercise 5 again. Then compare your ideas with other students.

Home | Forum | News | Sign in

Q We asked you, our readers, 'What invention or discovery would make your life better?' Here are some of your answers.

A clone. If I had a clone of myself, I would have so much more time. I'd send my clone to do all the boring stuff I don't like doing. He would take all my exams and he would wait in all those long boring queues for me. That would leave me more time to do the things I really want to do.

Oliver

I wish someone would find a way to stop me feeling tired in the mornings. It doesn't matter what time I go to bed, I never want to get out of bed the next morning, even at the weekends when I don't have to get up early for school. I'd stay in bed until the afternoon if I could. Life without an alarm clock – that would be perfect!

Eve

I wish I had a super-quick travel machine like they have in the *Star Trek* films. You know what I mean, a machine that could transport me anywhere in the world in seconds. So, imagine you're in one place. You enter some coordinates into the machine and two seconds later you're there. For example, you could have breakfast in Italy, visit the Amazon in the morning and spend the afternoon at the South Pole. If there was a machine like that, I'd visit the whole world.

Matthew

I want to be a scientist when I grow up, so the thing that I would like most is a huge laboratory underneath my house. A secret one that only I knew about. Down there I'd do lots of research and experiments. Then I would invent lots of different things that would make peoples' lives better, like cures for diseases. If anyone can help make my dream come true, please get in touch.

Aimee

GRAMMAR
Second conditional

9 Complete these sentences with the phrases in the list. Are the sentences about real or imagined situations?

would | could do | had | stay | there was | visit

1 If I ______ a clone of myself, I ______ have so much more time.
2 If ______ a machine like that, I'd ______ the whole world.
3 I'd ______ in bed until the afternoon if I ______ .

10 Complete the rules.

RULE: We use the second conditional to talk about the consequences of an unreal present action or [1]**a probable / an improbable** future action.
- Condition clause: ***if*** + [2]______ simple.
- Result clause: [3]______ / ***wouldn't*** (***would not***) + verb.

The condition clause can come before or after the result clause.

11 Choose the correct words.

0 If I *had* / *would have* a bit more time, I *went* / *would go* and see my friends tonight.
1 They *would learn* / *learned* more if they *would listen* / *listened* more carefully.
2 If my school *would be* / *was* a long way from home, I *would have* / *had* to take a bus.
3 He *lent* / *would lend* you his tablet if you *asked* / *would ask* him nicely.
4 If he *was* / *would be* really ill, he *stay* / *would stay* in bed.
5 I *gave* / *would give* you her address if I *knew* / *would know* it myself.

12 Complete the sentences with the correct form of the verbs.

0 I think it *'d be* (be) a great party if the food *was* (be) better.
1 Who ________ you ________ (talk) to if you ________ (have) a really serious problem?
2 She ________ (like) you if you ________ (be) nicer to her.
3 If his father ________ (not make) him tidy his room, he ________ (not do) it.
4 If you ________ (can) have any present you want, what ________ you ________ (choose)?

I wish

13 Read the sentences. How are they alike?

1 I wish someone would find a way to stop me feeling tired.
2 I wish I had a super-quick travel machine.

14 Complete the sentences with the correct form of the underlined verbs.

0 The bus isn't here. I wish the bus *was* here.
1 We aren't a good team. I wish we ______ a better team.
2 I can't go home. I wish I ______ go home.
3 It's raining. I wish it ______ raining.
4 They are making so much noise! I wish they ______ so much noise!

15 SPEAKING Work in pairs. Which person in the pictures is thinking which thing from Exercise 14? (More than one answer is possible.)

→ workbook page 73

VOCABULARY
Science

16 Match the words with the definitions.

1 ☐ a cure
2 ☐ to discover
3 ☐ an experiment
4 ☐ to invent
5 ☐ a laboratory
6 ☐ a machine
7 ☐ to do research
8 ☐ a scientist

a to study something
b someone who works in an area of science
c a room for scientific work
d something that makes a sick person well again
e to find something new
f a test to see if something works or is true
g to make something new
h a piece of equipment that does a specific kind of work

17 SPEAKING Work in pairs. What invention or discovery would make your life better? What invention or discovery would make the lives of all people better?

18 SPEAKING In class, compare everyone's ideas and vote for the best ones.

→ workbook page 74

Culture

THINK
Simple inventions

1 Look at the images. What can you see in each one?

2 8.06 Read and listen to the article about four inventions. Match the images with the inventions. Write 1–4 in the boxes.

AMAZING INVENTIONS FROM ANCIENT CIVILIZATIONS

Throughout history, humankind has progressed thanks to amazing inventions and discoveries. Some of the inventions we use in our everyday life are a lot older than you might think. Here are four of them.

1 Nanotechnology – *Ancient Italy*

The Lycurgus Cup is a beautifully decorated glass cup that was made in Italy in the fourth century.

For years, it confused scientists because it seems to change colour. When light shines through it from the front, it looks green, but when it shines from the back, it appears red. In the 1990s, scientists looked at the glass under a microscope. They discovered something amazing. Whoever had made the glass had used tiny pieces of gold and silver. Some of these pieces measured 50 nanometres across – about one-thousandth the size of a piece of salt. It is these tiny pieces that make the cup change colour. The Lycurgus Cup shows that the ancient Romans were using nanotechnology more than 1,600 years ago.

2 Earthquake detector – *Ancient China*

More than 2,000 years ago, an inventor called Zhang Heng built the world's first earthquake detector. The machine was a large metal vase on which there were eight dragon heads. The dragons marked the eight points of a compass, and each one had a metal ball in its mouth. Below each dragon head, there was a metal frog. When the machine detected tremors in the earth, one of the dragons (facing in the direction of the tremor) would drop its ball into the mouth of the frog that sat below it. This made a loud noise that warned people of the earthquake. The machine could detect earthquakes hundreds of kilometres away.

3 Electricity – *Iraq*

In 1936, during some excavations in an ancient village near Baghdad, an archaeologist found some unusual clay pots. The pots were more than 2,000 years old.

Hanging inside each pot was a copper cylinder and inside this cylinder was a piece of iron. Nobody knew why somebody had made these pots with metal inside, but the archaeologist thought that they could be some sort of early battery. A few years later American scientists made copies of the pots. They discovered that the original theory was right: they could make electricity. But why? What did people use this electricity for? That is the great mystery of this discovery.

4 The calendar – *Ancient Scotland*

Very early calendars from ancient civilizations have been found in many countries around the world. But archaeologists believe that they have discovered a calendar in Scotland that is 10,000 years old. It was made by Stone Age Britons, who used it from 8000 BCE to 4000 BCE. The calendar was made of 12 pits dug into the ground. The pits represented the months of the year and were laid out in a long line that was 50 metres long. The Ancient Britons would measure time using the sun and the moon. This ancient calendar used both to keep track of the days, weeks and months of the year.

A ☐

B ☐

C ☐

D ☐

3 **Read the article again and write the names of the countries next to the information.**

1 The item was discovered under the ground here. ______
2 The item found here was decorated with animals. ______
3 The invention let them know about a danger here. ______
4 The invention was used for 4,000 years here. ______
5 They used the moon here to mark the passing of the year. ______
6 The item discovered here kept its secret for a long time. ______
7 The item discovered here contained valuable metals. ______
8 We're not sure what the people here used the invention for. ______

4 VOCABULARY **There are eight highlighted words in the article. Match the words with these meanings.**

1 an instrument for looking closely at very small things ______
2 noticed or discovered, using special equipment ______
3 large holes in the earth ______
4 tube ______
5 movements of the earth ______
6 an idea (often about science) ______
7 science involving very very small things ______
8 someone who digs the earth to find objects from the past ______

5 SPEAKING **Which of the inventions do you think is the most important? Why? Share your ideas with the class.**

WRITING
A blog entry

1 INPUT **Ellen wrote a blog entry with the title 'A world without television'. Read what she wrote and answer the questions.**

1 What did people do before they had television?
2 What does Ellen think life would be like without TV?

2 ANALYSE **Look at Ellen's blog entry again.**

1 In which paragraph does Ellen use *used to*? In which does she use the second conditional? Why does she use them?

3 **Match the paragraphs with these headings.**

A Imagine life without television ☐
B Life before television ☐

4 **What type of text is Ellen's blog? Give reasons.**

- her personal opinion
- a fictional story
- a factual article
- an article for the school magazine

Ellen's blog

A WORLD WITHOUT TELEVISION

1 It isn't easy to imagine life without television, but people only started to have television at home about 60 years ago. So a lot of people who are alive today lived without it in the past. Before television, people used to read in the evening or listen to the radio. I read once that families used to get together and sing songs or tell each other stories. I think it was probably a bit boring but perhaps people enjoyed it.

2 If we didn't have television these days, I think things would be OK. I mean, we would still have films and the internet that we could watch on laptops, wouldn't we? We would get all the information and entertainment we need there, and in fact many people already do. I know a lot of people who don't watch television at all; they watch sport and things by streaming them. But of course, they're using TV programmes when they do that – so maybe a world without TV wouldn't be such a good idea!

5 PLAN **You are going to write a blog entry like Ellen's. Choose one of these pieces of technology, or use your own idea. Write a plan and make notes.**

mobile phones　tablets
the internet　calculators

6 PRODUCE **Write your blog entry. Write 120–180 words. Use your notes to help you.**

B1 Preliminary for Schools

READING

Part 1: 3-option multiple choice

→ workbook page 71

1 **For each question, choose the correct answer.**

1

The recent rain has made the school fields very wet and we might need to move the school sports day from Saturday to Sunday. Please see this notice board for further information.

1 What does the notice say?

A The sports day will now take place on Sunday.

B The weather will be bad this weekend.

C There is a chance the sports day will still take place on Saturday.

2

14:10

Hi Claudia – I want to start French lessons. You said John Gray teaches French. Have you got his email address so I can write to him? Best, Anna

2 Why has Anna sent this message?

A She wants Claudia to talk to John Gray.

B She would like to contact the French teacher.

C She wishes she could start French lessons.

3

Jemma – would it be OK if you didn't use any of the eggs? I need them to make a cake when I get back from work. By the way, try the soup – it's delicious. Thanks, Jim

3 What is Jim doing in this message?

A He's telling Jemma she can eat the soup but not the eggs.

B He's asking that Jemma avoid eating any eggs.

C He's saying Jemma can eat the cake.

4

PHOTOGRAPHY FOR BEGINNERS

5-week course starts Tuesday 5th Oct.

There are still a few places.

BOOK WITH STEVE

4 What's true about the photography course?

A The course is already full.

B Contact Steve if you are interested in learning more about the course.

C The course finishes at the end of October.

5

16:42

Hi Ashley, Really sorry to miss your party. Hope it's a lot of fun. Work is no fun at all! So boring and I'll finish late tonight. Fin

5 What is Fin telling Ashley?

A Fin wishes he could go to Ashley's party.

B Fin is going to be late for the party.

C Fin thinks that work is as fun as the party.

WRITING

Part 1: An email

2 **Read this email from your English-speaking friend Sam and the notes you have made.**

Write your email to Sam using all the notes. Write about 100 words.

→ workbook page 61

Science fair

Hi

Do you remember that we talked about going to the science fair? Our teacher suggested we should go.

Well, guess what! I've got two free tickets. Would you like to come with me? (← *accept*)

It's on all weekend. We can go Saturday or Sunday. I'm free on both days. As usual I've got nothing planned. What's best for you? (← *say which day*)

It's not far and there are transport options. (← *suggest a transport option*)

I'm free in the evening, too. Would you like to do anything after? (← *suggest*)

Let me know!

Sam

VOCABULARY

1 Complete the sentences with the words in the list. There are two extra words.

away | cure | experiment | hire | invitations | later
long | near | next | research | towards | up and down

1 Sorry, I can't come and see you this weekend – but how about the week after ____________________ ?
2 I got scared when the dog started running ____________________ me.
3 I'm going to do an ____________________ to see if my idea works.
4 I think we should send out ____________________ to everyone who we want to come.
5 I can't talk to you right now. Could you please phone me back ____________________ today?
6 It's my sister's 16th birthday next month, and we're going to ____________________ a DJ to play at the party.
7 He's got a serious disease, and the doctor says there's no ____________________ for it.
8 I'm going to do some ____________________ on the internet before I write my essay.
9 He was very late! I got a bit nervous and started walking ____________________ outside the school.
10 We're hoping to buy a bigger car in the ____________________ future.

/10

GRAMMAR

2 Complete the sentences. Put the verbs in brackets into the correct form or write the missing word(s).

1 I missed the train, so I ____________________ (take) a taxi home.
2 This lesson's really boring, ____________________ ?
3 I saw Sue while I ____________________ (walk) in town yesterday.
4 **A** I really don't like Kevin.
B ____________________ do I.
5 Your sister's got lots of clothes, ____________________ ?
6 **A** I hate Mondays.
B ____________________ do I.

3 Find and correct the mistake in each sentence.

1 When I was a kid, I used to playing with dolls.
2 If you would work harder, you would do better in your tests.
3 When you phoned me, I watched TV.
4 The world was a happier place if people laughed more.
5 Dan never watches football, and so do I.
6 I wish this question isn't so difficult!

/12

FUNCTIONAL LANGUAGE

4 Complete the mini-dialogues with the words in the list.

do | did | neither | so | used | wait | was | wish

1 **A** I can't ____________________ for the Ed Sheeran concert.
B ____________________ can I! It's going to be great.
2 **A** I ____________________ to love that film when I was a kid.
B So ____________________ I. I thought it was the best.
3 **A** I ____________________ it wasn't so windy.
B ____________________ do I. I want to go for a bike ride!
4 **A** Where's Paul? I wish he ____________________ here.
B So ____________________ I. Parties are always better with Paul.

/8

MY SCORE /30

22–30 | 10–21 | 0–9

9 WORKING WEEK

OBJECTIVES

FUNCTIONS:
accepting and refusing offers and invitations; inviting friends to join you

GRAMMAR:
the passive (present simple, past simple, present continuous, present perfect)

VOCABULARY:
jobs; *work as / in / for*; *work* vs. *job*; time expressions with *in*

Get THINKING

Watch the video and think: what kind of job do you want to have?

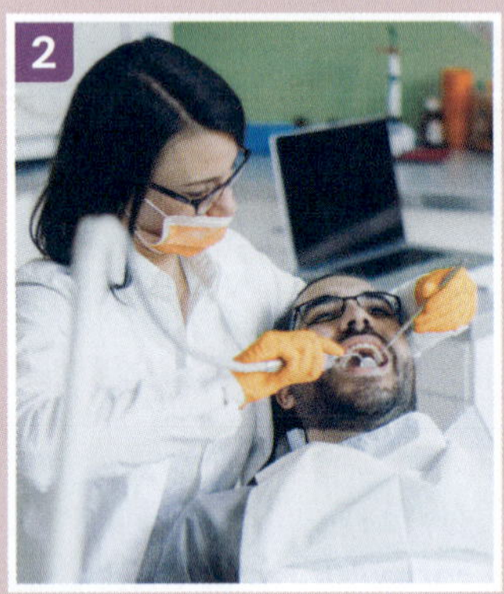

READING

1 **What jobs can you see in the photos? What other jobs can you name in English? With a partner, write down as many as you can.**

2 **Which of the jobs you thought of in Exercise 1 …**

1. sometimes involves work in the evening or at night?
2. needs a lot of training?
3. involves work at weekends?
4. is well paid?
5. gets a lot of holidays?
6. can be dangerous?

3 SPEAKING **Compare your ideas from Exercises 1 and 2 with others in the class.**

4 **Look at the photos on the next page. What jobs do you think the people have? Read the article quickly to check your ideas.**

5 9.01 **Read and listen to the article again and mark the sentences T (true) or F (false).**

1. Netflix employ about 30 professional film watchers. ____
2. A 'tag' consists of a small number of words describing a film. ____
3. Anyone who loves film can become a Netflix tagger. ____
4. The window-cleaners of the Gherkin use ropes to get to the top windows. ____
5. The window-cleaners work in all kinds of weather. ____
6. The cleaners use a special chemical to clean the windows. ____
7. You need to study at university to become a pet psychologist. ____
8. Pet psychologists can talk to animals. ____
9. A pet psychologist can help owners understand why their dog barks too loudly. ____

6 SPEAKING **Work in pairs. Correct the false sentences in Exercise 5.**

THE PERFECT JOB?

What would you choose as the perfect job? Here are three that could be on your list!

MOVIE MADNESS

For all big film fans out there, this is THE dream job. Most people pay to watch films, but in this job, YOU are paid to watch TV series and films. Around 30 people are employed by Netflix to watch Netflix content. They are required to binge-watch the latest films and TV series on the platform and 'tag' them with a few words. So, how does that work and why is it done? Words to describe each film or TV series are entered into the system. This is done so that Netflix users can search for content more easily. For example, in the sci-fi category, the tags include *future* and *planets*. The release date of the film, the language, the director and actors in the film are also included.

How do you become a Netflix tagger? Well, first you need to have worked in the film or TV industry for five years. You also need to specialise in a film category, for example, comedy, horror or teen movies. Then there is a very difficult interview for the job. All Netflix taggers must have an excellent knowledge of film and TV.

window-cleaners abseiling a skyscraper

ONLY DAREDEVILS NEED APPLY

Are you scared of heights? Then this is not the job for you. But if you are very brave and love rock climbing, then cleaning the windows of really tall skyscrapers is the perfect job for you. There is some on-the-job training to clean the windows: the cleaners are taught to abseil down from the top of the buildings. That means they move down the outside of the windows held by a rope around their bodies.

Imagine cleaning the windows of the famous London Gherkin! It's 180 metres tall and 40 storeys high. It was designed by a very famous English architect and it was built in the 2000s. Cleaners abseil down to the 35th floor. Below the 35th floor, the cleaners can work in a traditional cradle.

It takes nine of them ten days to clean the whole building. Cleaners don't work on days when the winds are too strong. And guess what? The Gherkin is cleaned with soap and water.

Where do the cleaners go for lunch? Well, lunch breaks aren't taken in a café. They are taken sitting at the top of the 40-storey building. Imagine that amazing view every day.

PET PSYCHOLOGIST

If you love animals, this could be the dream job for you. The pay is good, too. You can earn between £25,000 and £50,000 per year.

The job is to study animal behaviour and help owners discover the causes of their pets' problems. To work as a pet psychologist, you need to have a degree in veterinary science or zoology. You also need experience of working with animals, for example at a vet's or at a zoo.

So, how is the job done? First, they talk to the owner to find out about the problem with the pet. For example, it may run after cars or bark too loudly. Then the animal is observed by the psychologist, and afterwards, once the pet psychologist discovers the causes of the pet's problems, the owners are given advice about how to help their pets.

THINK values

What's important in a job?

7 What do you think about the jobs in the text? Tick (✓) the boxes.

	Netflix tagger	Extreme window-cleaner	Pet psychologist
1 This job is a waste of time.	☐	☐	☐
2 This job sounds fun.	☐	☐	☐
3 This job didn't exist in the past.	☐	☐	☐
4 This job is dangerous.	☐	☐	☐
5 I would like to have this job.	☐	☐	☐

8 SPEAKING Compare your ideas with others in the class.

9 Think of a job you might like to do in the future and write it down. Look at values a–f below. Rank each one 1–6 (1 = low, 6 = high) for your job.

Job:

Value	Score
a You can make a lot of money.	
b You might become famous.	
c It helps people.	
d It's fun to do.	
e It gives you lots of free time.	
f It's creative.	

10 SPEAKING Talk to others in your class. Compare your job and values with theirs.

Grammar rap!

GRAMMAR
The passive: present simple and past simple

1 Complete these sentences from the article on page 85. Then choose the correct options to complete the rules about the passive.

1 Around 30 people ______ (employ) by Netflix to watch Netflix content.
2 The Gherkin ______ (design) by a very famous English architect.
3 It ______ (build) in the 2000s.
4 Lunch breaks ______ (not take) in a café.
5 The animal ______ (observe) by the psychologist.
6 The owners ______ (give) advice about how to help their pets.

RULE: Form the passive with the verb [7]**to be / to have** + the past participle of the main verb.
We use the passive when
- it [8]**is / isn't** important who does or did the action.
- we [9]**want / don't want** to focus on the action itself and not the person doing it.
- we [10]**know / don't know** who does or did the action.

2 Complete the sentences with the present simple passive or past simple passive form of the verbs.

0 Every year, hundreds of films *are made* (make) in Hollywood.
1 It was interesting work, but she ___________ (not pay) very much money.
2 Tigers ___________ (not find) in Africa.
3 This novel ___________ (write) a hundred years ago.
4 Lots of new websites ___________ (design) especially for small children.
5 When ___________ the Mona Lisa ___________ (paint)?
6 In the US, the president ___________ (choose) every four years.
7 ___________ you ___________ (ask) to help with the party?
8 Why ___________ permission ___________ (not give) for the party?

PRONUNCIATION
/tʃ/ and /dʒ/ consonant sounds Go to page 121.

3 How many passive sentences can you make? (Your sentences can be positive or negative.)

Millions of pizzas	build	fifty years ago
The World Cup	buy	every day
How many emails	eat	last night
Our house	discover	in 1492
America	make	in China
This email	play	to me by mistake
How many songs	send	every four years
This book	write	two years ago

→ workbook page 82

VOCABULARY
Jobs

4 Read the essay. Which jobs does the writer talk about?

My first job was as a waiter. I did it when I first left school, just **to earn** money. It was fun, but it was very hard work. I had **to work long hours** and I was always on my feet! It wasn't very **challenging** – I had to remember the customers' orders, but that was all. And I didn't **get paid holidays**.

So, in the end I got bored and I **gave in my notice** and got a job as a shop assistant in a bookshop. I really enjoyed that because I like books and I like talking to people about them. After a few months I was **promoted** to shop manager. That was great! I got **on-the-job training** about management, and I was happy because I was **starting a career** – well, I thought I was. After two years, the bookstore closed because there wasn't enough business.

Now I've got a few more years' experience, and I work as a management consultant. **The pay** is fantastic and the work is quite interesting. I guess you can say I'm **successful**. Will I still be here five years from now? Who knows? Anything could happen in the next few years.

5 Match the bold expressions in Exercise 4 with their definitions. Write the words.

0 the money you get for doing a job *the pay*
1 to get money for doing a job ___________
2 given a higher position ___________
3 beginning a job (or series of jobs) that you might do for life ___________
4 achieving a lot, and/or making a lot of money ___________
5 be paid for the days that you don't work ___________
6 said you didn't want a job any more ___________
7 to work many hours every day ___________
8 a way of learning to do a job at the same time that you do it ___________
9 difficult in a way that tests your abilities ___________

6 **Look at these jobs. Which sentences can be used to describe each job? (There's often more than one possibility.) Compare your ideas with others in your class.**

1 You have to work long hours.
2 The pay can be excellent.
3 If you're good at the job, you might be promoted.
4 It's a very good career.
5 It's not challenging at all.
6 The only reason to do this job is to earn money.
7 If you're successful in this job, you could be famous.
8 You can do this job with on-the-job training.

→ workbook page 84

LISTENING

7 **Look at the pictures of these people. Match the words to the pictures.**

1 blind 2 deaf 3 in a wheelchair

8 SPEAKING **Here are some jobs. Do you think that the people in Exercise 7 could do all of these jobs?**

1 teacher
2 actor
3 musician
4 pilot
5 shop assistant
6 taxi driver

I think a person in a wheelchair can be a teacher or an actor.

9 9.04 **Listen to a programme with a woman called Marina Stuart. Choose the correct answers.**

1 Marina is …
A deaf.
B blind.
C in a wheelchair.

2 Marina works as …
A an actor.
B a piano teacher.
C an actor and a piano teacher.

10 9.04 **Listen again and answer the questions.**

1 What happened to Marina when she was 18?
2 What were the teachers like at her college?
3 Why didn't she leave the job that she hated?
4 Who did Marina meet by accident?
5 How many of the films she was in won an award?
6 Why does Marina think she has been successful?

WordWise: Time expressions with *in*

11 **Complete the sentences from the unit so far with a phrase from the list.**

in the end | in the next few years | in the past

1 This job didn't exist ________________ .
2 ________________ I got bored and gave in my notice.
3 Anything could happen ________________ .

12 **Match the questions and answers.**

1 When's your birthday? ☐
2 Can we go out tomorrow? ☐
3 When will you see your grandparents? ☐
4 Is it hot in your country? ☐
5 When's your next exam? ☐

a Yes, let's meet up *in* the evening.
b It's *in* two weeks' time. I'll be 15.
c *In* the summer holidays, I hope.
d I'm not really sure but I think it's *in* June.
e Yes, *in* the summer.

13 SPEAKING **Work with a partner. Answer the questions in Exercise 12 so that they are true for you.**

→ workbook page 84

READING

1 **Look at the photos. Which of these people work in …**

1 the entertainment industry?
2 law enforcement?
3 the catering industry?
4 journalism?

2 9.05 **Read and listen to the article. Answer the questions.**

1 What types of articles are computers able to write?
2 How many film trailers did IBM's supercomputer Watson study?
3 How quickly did Watson make a film trailer?
4 What does the cheese and chocolate panini suggest about computers in the kitchen?
5 How can the public interact with the robocop?

3 SPEAKING **Think of two jobs that you believe will exist in 30 years. They could be jobs that don't exist yet today, or jobs that will always be necessary. Tell others in the class and explain why.**

I think composers will still be needed in 30 years. Robots won't have the creativity to write original music.

WRITING
A short essay

4 **Write a short essay about your ideas from Exercise 3. Describe the jobs and explain why you believe they will exist in the future.**

1

2

3

4

TECHNOLOGY in the workplace

The world is being taken over by computers. They are doing jobs in seconds that once took us hours to do and they are helping us to do things we once only ever dreamed of doing. Advances in AI (artificial intelligence) and robotics mean that computers have become better at doing difficult tasks and can even teach themselves how to do them. As more and more jobs are being done by computers maybe it's time to start asking – are any of our jobs safe in the future? Here are four which might be in danger.

JOURNALISTS

Are you planning to work in journalism one day? If the answer is yes, you need to be aware that journalists who write articles based on numbers and data, such as business or sports journalists, may lose their jobs to robots in the future. Some short sports articles have already been written by a computer program. However, robots are not good at being creative. They need numbers and data that they can then describe and aren't able to write descriptive articles. So, while some types of journalism jobs may go, those who write more creative articles should be safe from computers taking over their jobs.

TRAILER MAKERS

The first AI film trailer, for a horror film, has been made by a computer. The supercomputer, IBM's Watson, learned how to make one by looking at 100 trailers from other horror films. These were analysed by the supercomputer and it learned how to produce a film trailer. It then watched 20th Century Fox's film, *Morgan*, to find the right moments to include in the trailer. Instead of taking 10 to 30 days to make the trailer, it only took 24 hours.

CHEFS

Can robots cook? The answer to this question is: not yet. Robots cannot prepare, cook or serve full meals, but an AI machine has been trained to create recipes. If you give it information about the ingredients and style of cooking you want, it will give you some ideas for different meals. This could be very useful. Especially when you only have a few things in the cupboard. However, it's not perfect yet. A journalist asked it for a 'Chinese-style' dish with Parmesan cheese and dark chocolate. It suggested a cheese and chocolate panini. Maybe it needs a bit more development before it can work as a chef!

POLICE OFFICERS

Have you seen the sci-fi film *RoboCop*? In one country, fiction may become reality as people may soon see these robot police officers on the streets. A robocop has been developed in the United Arab Emirates and there are robocops working for the police force in Dubai.

These officers cannot solve crimes. However, people can report crimes to them. They have a touchscreen on their chests. People can pay their traffic fines to them, too. They have been designed to be friendly, so they will shake hands with people.

Dubai wants 25% of their police officers to be robots by 2030. They also want to have a smart police station, which will not employ any humans.

GRAMMAR

The passive: present continuous and present perfect

5 **Complete the sentences from the article on page 88 with the words in the list. Then complete the rules.**

are being | has been | have been | is being

1 The world ______ taken over by computers.
2 More and more jobs ______ done by computers.
3 Some short sports articles ______ already ______ written by a computer program.
4 The first AI film trailer, for a horror film, ______ made by a computer.

RULE: The passive is formed using the verb [5]______ + the past participle of the main verb.

- Form the present continuous passive (like sentences [6]______ and [7]______ above) using *is/are being* + past participle.
- Form the present perfect passive (like sentences [8]______ and [9]______ above) using *has/have been* + past participle.

6 **Complete the sentences with the present continuous passive or present perfect passive form of the verbs.**

0 For the last 30 years, the internet *has been used* (use) by people all over the world.
1 New machines ______________ (design) all the time.
2 Some jobs ______________ (take over) by computers.
3 A lot of new medicines ______________ (develop) in the last 50 years.
4 At the moment, thousands of new cars ______________ (build) around the world.
5 From January 1st until now, billions of mobile phone calls ______________ (make).
6 This new plane ______________ (test) over 200 times.

7 **Look at the pictures and make sentences about what is being done and what has been done.**

New doors have been added.

→ workbook page 83

VOCABULARY

work as / in / for

8 **Read the sentences. Then match the verbs with the objects.**

Are you planning to work in journalism one day?
It needs a bit more development before it can work as a chef.
There are robocops working for the police force in Dubai.

1 work in — a a person in a job
2 work as — b a company, person or organisation
3 work for — c an industry

9 **Complete the sentences with *as*, *in* or *for*.**

When my mother was young, she worked [1]______ a waitress to earn some money. After that, she was a secretary. She worked [2]______ some lawyers. Now she works [3]______ the computer industry.
My friend left school two years ago and got a job. She worked [4]______ a tour guide for about six months and really liked it. So she decided she wanted to work [5]______ the travel industry. Now she works [6]______ a travel agent in Australia.
My father works [7]______ television now. He works [8]______ a cameraman. He works [9]______ the biggest television company in the country.

Look

job is a countable noun – we can use it in the plural.
*She did four **jobs** before she became a travel agent.*
work is an uncountable noun – we don't use it in the plural.
*I have a lot of **work** to do tonight.*

work vs. *job*

10 **Complete the sentences with *work* or *job(s)*.**

0 She left school and got a *job* .
1 Sorry, I can't talk right now, I've got a lot of ______ to do on this project.
2 When the factory closed, my uncle lost his ______ as a manager.
3 I've got a new ______ in a bank.
4 My mother is the manager of a shop. She loves her ______ because it's very interesting ______ .
5 There aren't enough ______ in this town.
6 Being a street cleaner is very hard ______ .
7 Sometimes I have to take ______ home at the weekend.
8 Cleaning out the garage is a big ______ for one person.

→ workbook page 84

DEVELOPING SPEAKING

1 🔊 9.06 **Look at the photo. What do you think the dialogue will be about? Listen and read to check.**

Mrs Ashton: Hello, Andy. Your father was telling me that you want to earn some extra pocket money.
Andy: Hi, Mrs Ashton. That's right. I want to buy a new skateboard.
Mrs Ashton: Well, would you like to sort out my garage? It hasn't been tidied for years. I'll pay you £20 for two hours' work, as long as you do a good job.
Andy: Yes, that sounds great! Thank you. I'll start right away!
Mrs Ashton: OK, you'll find everything you need in the shed. I'm going out for a while, so you'll be on your own. By the way, some of those boxes are a bit heavy!
Andy: Don't worry, Mrs Ashton, I'll be careful.
Mrs Ashton: All right then. I'll see you soon. Have fun!
Two hours later …
Mrs Ashton: Hello, Andy. My goodness! The garage looks fantastic now. You've done a great job. Thank you.
Andy: I'm glad you like it. But I have to tell you something. I broke a vase.
Mrs Ashton: Oh no! Andy! Surely you haven't broken it! I loved that vase. It was worth a lot of money!
Andy: I'm really sorry, Mrs Ashton. It was an accident. I didn't mean to break it.
Mrs Ashton: That's not the point, Andy. My vase is broken! But anyway – here's your £20, and here's another £2 for being honest.
Andy: I don't understand! I broke your vase and you're going to pay me extra?
Mrs Ashton: You worked hard and you told me what happened. So, you've got your money and I've got a nice, tidy garage!

2 Read the dialogue again and answer the questions.

1 Why does Andy want to do some work?
2 What does Mrs Ashton say about the boxes?
3 What did Andy break?
4 Why does Mrs Ashton pay Andy £22 and not £20?

3 SPEAKING **Discuss the statements in pairs.**

1 Andy did the right thing to tell her about the vase.
2 Andy told her about the vase because he knew she'd give him more money.
3 Mrs Ashton shouldn't give Andy money for being honest.

Phrases for fluency

4 Find the underlined expressions in the dialogue and use them to complete the conversation.

A Hey. Let's have a party on Saturday. We haven't had a party [1]______________, have we?
B [2]______________! Where?
A Well, I thought perhaps … my place.
B Really? I thought your parents were really strict.
A Yes, they are, usually.
B [3]______________ they'll be OK with a small party.
A Well, I think so, [4]______________ it really *is* a small party. [5]______________, I'm not going to invite Alison. We had a *big* argument yesterday.
B You can tell your parents that the party won't go on late.
A [6]______________. My parents just don't like a lot of noise.

FUNCTIONS
Accepting and refusing offers and invitations

KEY LANGUAGE
Yes, I'd love to.
Sorry, no. But thanks for asking me.
I'm [really] sorry, I'm afraid I can't.
Yes, I'll [come along / join you / be there].

5 Put the expressions from the Key Language box inthe correct columns.

Accepting (saying yes)	Refusing (saying no)
Yes, that sounds great.	No, sorry, not this time.
[1]______________	[3]______________
______________	______________
[2]______________	[4]______________
______________	______________

6 SPEAKING **Work in pairs. Tell your partner about the last time you accepted or refused an invitation.**

ROLE PLAY Inviting friends to join you

Work in pairs. Student A: Go to page 127. Student B: Go to page 128. Role play the conversations. Invent more short dialogues to practise.

LIFE COMPETENCIES

It isn't easy to tell other people when we've made a mistake. We might worry about what they will do or say. But taking responsibility for our actions often means that other people will know to respect and trust us.

1 ▶ 27 **Watch the video. What did Anna's mum already know about her daughter?**

2 ▶ 27 **Watch again. Who said (or thought about saying) these things and why?**

1 Can I copy your homework? ______
2 Why haven't you done your homework? ______
3 The hamster ate it. ______
4 You never had a plate. ______
5 Sorry, but I've had a little accident. ______

3 **Amy is telling her friend about an exam she has failed. What excuses does she give for not studying?**

'Mum and Dad are going to be really angry with me. You know what? They'll probably say I can't visit my cousins in the holidays, and they'll make me study instead. It isn't fair. Mr Jones never gives me good marks. He just doesn't like me.

I didn't have time to study either. It was my birthday at the weekend. I had a party on Saturday evening and I spent all day organising it. I had to tell people what time to meet at the cinema, and I had to call the pizza place to get a table. Then on Sunday, people were messaging me all day to wish me a happy birthday. You can't just turn your phone off when people are being nice enough to message you, can you?

And then it was the first episode of *Lost Kings* on Sunday night, and I was too tired to study after that. Then this morning, I was late for school. Mum forgot to leave me money for the bus so I had to walk to school.'

4 SPEAKING **Work in pairs. Discuss these questions with your partner.**

1 Do you think any of Amy's excuses are good reasons for not studying?
2 Do you think it would be fair if Amy's parents punished her?
3 What should Amy say to her parents when they ask why she didn't study?
4 Do you sometimes blame other people when things go wrong? Do you think you're always right when you do?

Me and my world

5 **Here are some common excuses. Can you think of a time when you have said any of these things? Tell your partner about what happened.**

I didn't see it.	The teacher never told me.
Homework? What homework!?	She was doing it, so I did it, too.
It just broke.	I can't find it.
He started it.	They made me do it.

6 SPEAKING **Think about your answers to Exercise 5. What might be a more responsible thing to say if you're in a similar situation again? Share your ideas with a partner.**

TIPS FOR TAKING RESPONSIBILITY FOR YOUR ACTIONS

- Try to speak directly to someone when telling them what you've done. If you can't do that, write a letter or an email.
- Don't be surprised if the person you need to talk to is angry or upset at first. Stay calm. They will calm down and will respect you for being honest.
- Be sincere. Don't make excuses – just say what happened.

10 MIND AND BODY

OBJECTIVES

FUNCTIONS:
talking about your health

GRAMMAR:
past perfect simple; past perfect continuous; past perfect simple vs. past perfect continuous

VOCABULARY:
time linkers; illness: collocations

Get THINKING

Watch the video and think: how healthy is your lifestyle?

1

3

2

4

READING

1 SPEAKING **Work in pairs. Look at the photos and name the free-time activities. What other activities can you think of?**

2 **Think about the activities you discussed in Exercise 1. Answer the question and take notes.**

How might each of these free-time activities be good for someone's health?

3 SPEAKING **Discuss your answers with your partner.**

Cooking your own food can be good for your health. You can choose fresh ingredients so the food is better for you.

4 **Look at the photos on the next page. What do you think the text is about? Read the text quickly to check your ideas.**

5 **Read the sentences. Five of them were taken out of the text. Write the numbers 1–7 in the boxes. There are two sentences you don't need.**

1 By now she was becoming internationally famous in the birdwatching world.
2 It's not a very beautiful bird and it's not easy to find.
3 Snetsinger had become a legend.
4 She had less than a year to live.
5 She was there enjoying the hobby that had probably saved her life.
6 There were very few countries she hadn't visited.
7 This helped her remain healthy for another ten years.

6 10.01 **Read and listen to the article again to check your answers.**

8,000 BIRDS TO SEE BEFORE YOU DIE

Phoebe Snetsinger had just returned from a trip to Alaska when her doctors told her that she had cancer. **A** ☐ Phoebe was 50. As soon as she heard the news, she decided to spend the rest of her life doing what she loved most – watching birds.

Phoebe's interest in birdwatching started in Minneapolis. Then she moved to Missouri with her family. There she joined a group of people who were interested in birds, insects and plants around the Mississippi River. She became very worried about pollution and its impact on the environment. 'We have to protect nature,' she said. 'If we don't, future generations won't be able to enjoy watching these beautiful birds.'

When Phoebe found out she had cancer, she immediately went off to some of the world's most amazing natural paradises. Her trips were extremely hard, but Phoebe surprised her doctors and her family as she carried on travelling. A year came and went, and she was still alive. She was doing something that she loved. **B** ☐

The cancer came back, but even then Phoebe Snetsinger decided not to stop. As she continued with her trips, the cancer went away again. **C** ☐ At the age of 61, when she had seen 7,530 species, she was named 'the world's leading bird-spotter' by the Guinness Book of Records.

Four years later, during a trip to Mexico, she set a new record when she spotted species number 8,000: the very rare Rufous-necked Wood-Rail. **D** ☐ Nobody had spotted so many different bird species before. In fact, at that time only 12 people around the world had seen more than 7,000 species of birds!

Sadly, when Phoebe was 68, she died in a car accident on the island of Madagascar. **E** ☐ She had been there for two weeks and had added another five to her list of over 8,400 species. Four years after she died, the American Birding Association published her memoirs, *Birding on Borrowed Time*. Many people have enjoyed reading this moving book. It isn't just a story about a bird-spotter's travels, but a touching human document of how her hobby helped her to live much longer than expected.

TH!NK values

Never give up

7 **Tick (✓) the sentences that show what you think you can learn from this story.**

- ☐ Being passionate about things you like is extremely important.
- ☐ A hobby you really like can have a positive effect on your health.
- ☐ It's important to have friends you can trust at all times.
- ☐ You should always think positively and never give up hope.
- ☐ It's very important to eat healthy food and take enough exercise.

8 SPEAKING **Work in pairs. Compare your answers to Exercise 7.**

9 SPEAKING **Which of the sentences that you ticked in Exercise 7 is the most important one for you? Give reasons. Tell your partner.**

GRAMMAR
Past perfect simple

1 Read the example sentences and answer the questions. Then complete the rules.

*Phoebe Snetsinger **had** just **returned** from a trip to Alaska when her doctors **told** her that she had cancer.*

1 Which of the two actions came first: her returning from a trip or the doctors telling her she had cancer?

*Four years later she **set** a new record. Nobody **had spotted** so many different bird species.*

2 Which action came first?

RULE: When we tell a story, we often use the past perfect to talk about one event that happened before another event in the past.
She died in a car accident on the island of Madagascar. She had been there for two weeks.
(She was there for two weeks before she died.)

had been there — *died*
PAST — (two weeks) — NOW

Form the past perfect with *had* (or *'d*) + the [3]_______________ of the verb.

2 Complete the sentences. Use the past perfect form of the verbs.

1 When I tried to phone them, nobody answered. They ______ all ______ (go) swimming.
2 He ______ (change) so much that I almost didn't recognise him when I saw him last night.
3 She couldn't phone me because she ______ (lose) her mobile.
4 Somebody ______ (steal) John's car, so he was very angry.
5 Claire had no idea I was coming to see her. Her mum ______ (forget) to tell her.
6 You arrived too late. They ______ already ______ (leave).
7 Her mother ______ (not give) her any money so she couldn't buy the tickets.
8 ______ they already ______ (return) from their holiday when you got to their house?

3 Think about times in the past when you experienced a strong emotion. Then complete these sentences with your own words. Use the past perfect.

1 I was really sad because …
2 I was absolutely delighted when I found out that …
3 I was angry when …
4 I was very tired after …

→ workbook page 90

VOCABULARY
Time linkers

4 Read the story. Complete it with the words in the list.

as soon as | then | until | when | while

When I was a child, I was never really very interested in nature. [1]______ one day my aunt gave me a book for my birthday. It was called *Birding on Borrowed Time* by a woman called Phoebe Snetsinger. [2]______ she gave it to me I was a little disappointed. It didn't seem very interesting, and I wanted a new game for my games console. My aunt made me promise to read it. So I did, and I loved it. It was so interesting. [3]______ I was reading the book, I completely forgot about time. In fact, I didn't do anything else [4]______ I'd finished it – no TV, no gaming, nothing. [5]______ I had finished the book, I went out and bought myself a pair of binoculars. And that's how my interest in birdwatching started.

5 Match the parts of the sentence.

1 I never really liked Annie *until* ☐
2 *As soon as* I saw John's face ☐
3 *When* we got home after school ☐
4 *While* I was riding my bike ☐
5 I read the whole letter. *Then* ☐

a we did our homework immediately.
b I saw it wasn't for me.
c I realised we have a lot in common.
d I noticed something was wrong with it.
e I knew he was really worried.

6 Complete the sentences so that they are true for you.

1 While I was walking to school this morning …
2 The first thing I did when I arrived at home yesterday …
3 I had never eaten any … until …
4 As soon as I learned how to (swim / play the violin / write my name …), …
5 I heard my favourite singer for the first time in … . Then …

→ workbook page 92

LISTENING

7 10.02 **Listen to Lucas and Jackie talking. Jackie is going to the gym. Mark the sentences T (true) or F (false).**

1 Lucas has never been to a gym. ______
2 Jackie and Lucas go into the shopping centre together. ______
3 Lucas goes into the gym with Jackie. ______

8 10.02 **Listen again. At home Lucas tries to remember what Jackie said. He writes some things down but can't remember everything. Complete his notes for him.**

What Jackie said:

- Walking fast is good for your [1] ______________ .
- Dancing is good exercise.
- It's better to use the [2] ______________ than the escalator.
- One really bad thing is to [3] ______________ and [4] ______________ at the same time because then the food [5] ______________ you so much good.
- A good exercise to do every day is the [6] ______________ .

9 Which of these pictures shows the exercise Jackie mentions?

A

B

C

D

10 SPEAKING **Work in pairs. What's your opinion of the things Jackie says about exercise?**

Train to TH!NK

Logical conclusions

11 Complete the sentences from the conversation with *so* and *should*. Then decide in which of the sentences the speaker makes a suggestion and in which the speaker draws a conclusion.

a I feel much better afterwards, ______ I go to the gym every week.
b You ______ walk as much as you can, and sometimes walk quite fast.

Look

A conclusion is only valid if it follows logically from the information given. If we need to make assumptions about facts that are not part of the information, then the conclusion is invalid.

12 SPEAKING **Which of these conclusions are valid? Which are invalid? Give reasons.**

A Most kinds of sports are good for your health.
Car racing is a sport.
Therefore car racing is good for your health.
valid ☐ invalid ☐

B Spending time outdoors in the fresh air is good for your health.
Birdwatching is done outdoors in the fresh air.
Therefore, birdwatching is a healthy free-time activity.
valid ☐ invalid ☐

C Vitamins are good for the immune system.
Fruit has got vitamins in it.
Therefore eating fruit is good for the immune system.
valid ☐ invalid ☐

D Positive thinking can be good for your health.
John is a positive thinker.
John will never fall ill.
valid ☐ invalid ☐

The conclusion in A is invalid. It's true that most kinds of sports are good for your health. It's also true that car racing is a sport. But it's not true that all sports are good for your health. The first sentence talks about most kinds of sports, not all sports.

READING

1 **Look at the photos in the article. What do the dog and the girl have in common?**

2 SPEAKING **Work in pairs. Student A reads Story A; Student B reads Story B. Then tell your partner about the story you have read.**

3D PRINTING

IT CAN CHANGE LIVES

Prosthetics are artificial body parts. They're used by doctors to replace limbs (arms or legs) that are missing or have been damaged. For years, scientists had been making the prosthetics out of metal – steel at first, then lighter materials later. Recently, people have been using 3D printers to make prosthetics. Here are two stories of how lives were changed by 3D-printed prosthetics.

A

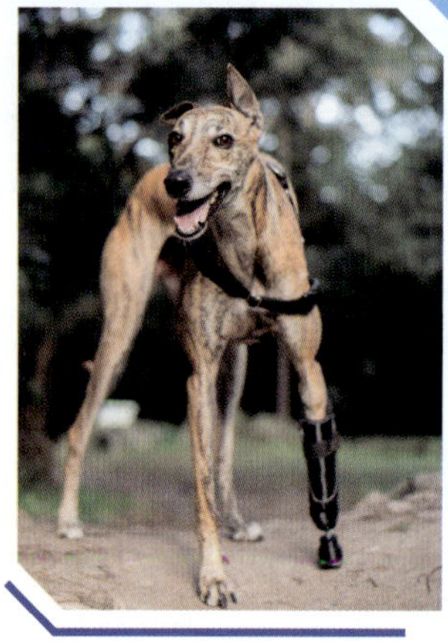

When Millie the greyhound was a puppy, she was in an accident and she lost her left front paw. Her first owner left her at a rescue centre, where Ed and Nora Dieppe found her and took her home. So that Millie could walk, her new owners put a prosthetic on her leg, but Millie soon wore it down and they had to replace it. Ed and Nora bought another prosthetic, but they soon had to replace that one, too. After a few years, they had spent over $10,000 on prosthetics. They wanted to help Millie, but they had to find a different way to do it.

Ed works as an architect. He had been working for some time with 3D modelling, and he had an idea. He talked to a company that helped him design a paw that would fit Millie perfectly. They then printed the leg using a 3D printer. They had to make two or three before the leg fitted perfectly, but soon they had a leg for Millie to wear. Now Millie can run around like other dogs, and if her leg wears out, Ed and Nora can just print a new one for her.

B

Stephen Davies was born without the lower part of his left arm. When he was at school, he wore a prosthetic, which he hated, so for many years he didn't wear a prosthetic at all. One day, he looked at what prosthetic arms were available. He saw that they hadn't changed much from when he was a boy. You could buy better ones, but they were extremely expensive.

That's OK for adults as they can use the same prosthetic arm for years. Children, though, need to change their prosthetic arm every few months because they grow so quickly. Stephen decided to do something. He had been creating lots of inventions in his garden shed. He had read that it was possible to print light, 3D prosthetics and he wondered if he could make them himself. He experimented with simple but very colourful arms and legs. He discovered that he could make good prosthetic limbs quite cheaply.

Now he and his business partner produce 'cool' limbs. Their company is called Team UnLimbited, and they give prosthetics away to children who need them (they ask for money on the internet to help with the costs of making the limbs). One of the first kids to get a 'cool' limb was nine-year-old Isabella Jennings. She had been waiting all her life for something like this. A video of her using the prosthetic arm for the first time was put on YouTube. It was watched by more than 2 million people.

3 10.03 **Read and listen to both stories. Mark the sentences A (Story A) or B (Story B).**

1 He didn't like his prosthetic at all. ______
2 The artificial limb had to be replaced several times. ______
3 They found a solution with 3D printing. ______
4 She can run and play now. ______
5 They make simple prosthetics that are free. ______
6 It was what she had always wanted. ______

GRAMMAR
Past perfect continuous

4 Complete these sentences from the stories on page 96. Choose the correct words to complete the rules.

1 He ______ (work) for some time with 3D modelling.
2 Stephen ______ (create) lots of inventions in his garden shed.
3 She ______ (wait) all her life for something like this.

> **RULE:** The past perfect continuous is used for actions happening over a period of time. We can use it
> - to talk about things that started in the [4]**present** / **past** and continued until another time in the past.
> - to talk about things that have stopped and had a result in the [5]**present** / **past**.
> - to focus on [6]**how long** / **how often** an activity had been happening.

5 Complete the sentences with the past perfect continuous form of the verbs in the list.

climb | not pay | try | wait | walk

1 I arrived late. They ______ for two hours.
2 They ______ for half an hour before they realised they'd left the picnic at the hotel.
3 Our teacher got very impatient with Thomas because he ______ attention at all that day.
4 We ______ to get tickets all afternoon, but the match was sold out by noon.
5 They looked exhausted when I saw them at the top. How long ______ they ______ ?

Past perfect simple vs. past perfect continuous

6 Complete the sentences with the past perfect simple or continuous form of the verbs.

1 I got to my friend's house at three o'clock. They ______ already ______ football for hours. (play)
2 Before the match started, it ______ for a long time. (rain)
3 I looked at my laptop and saw that somebody ______ it. (break)
4 She ______ Spanish for years when she went to university. (study)
5 My dad got home late. He told me that there ______ an accident on the motorway. (be)

→ workbook page 91

VOCABULARY
Illness: collocations

7 Match the sentence halves. Then underline the illness collocation in each sentence.

0 My dad hasn't <u>taken</u> any [d]
1 Our neighbour is in hospital. He had an [ ]
2 Her doctor gave her medication and she got [ ]
3 If you have a problem with your eyes, make an [ ]
4 Are you sure it's a cold? Maybe you should see [ ]
5 I ate seafood for dinner. I've been feeling [ ]

a better immediately.
b a doctor.
c appointment with a specialist soon!
d <u>exercise</u> for years now. He's not very healthy.
e sick all night.
f operation two days ago.

8 Complete the sentences with illness collocations from Exercise 7. Use the correct forms of the verbs.

1 I was really happy I could go to your party on Sunday. I ______ for almost a week.
2 Her knee hurts badly, and the medication she takes doesn't help. The doctors say she needs to ______ .
3 'Hello, this is Jake Miller. Can I ______ with Dr Thacker, please?'
4 I've got an earache, but I don't think it's too serious. If it's not gone in a few days I'll ______ .
5 The doctor says I'm a bit overweight and I should ______ some ______ every day.
6 Sorry to hear you're not feeling well. Hope you ______ soon.

→ workbook page 92

PRONUNCIATION
/tʃ/ and /ʃ/ consonant sounds Go to page 121.

FUNCTIONS
Talking about your health

9 SPEAKING **Work in pairs. Ask and answer questions.**

1 Have you ever felt sick after eating something? What happened?
2 When you have a cold, what do you do to get better?
3 Do you believe that taking exercise is good for you personally? Give reasons.
4 Where you live, is it easy or difficult to make an appointment with a doctor?
5 When you have a slight temperature, do you immediately see a doctor, or do you wait a few days?

TH!NK

A different sport?

Culture

1 **Look at the photos. Where do you think these activities take place?**

KEEP IN SHAPE

... WITHOUT GOING TO THE GYM!

Most people would like to be in good shape, but maybe without having to buy membership to a gym or go out cycling in all kinds of weather. There are so many different options these days to keep fit, while doing something you enjoy. Here are three of our favourites.

1 PARKRUN

Running is, of course, great exercise. Back in 2004, a group of 13 runners near London decided to meet up in their local park on Saturday mornings, every week, and run five kilometres. This has grown into an organisation known as ParkRun – and now there are ParkRun events in over twenty countries. In 2018, there were on average about 250,000 people running five kilometres in 1,500 events worldwide every Saturday.

Anyone can register to run: you do it online, and then turn up. Everyone's position and time is recorded, but even though it's a race, a ParkRun event is more about promoting good health and a sense of community. ParkRun is about everyone running 5 km, every week, for free, and forever.

2 ZUMBA

In the mid-1990s, a Colombian dancer called Beto Perez devised a workout programme that was a mixture of aerobics and dancing. He called it Zumba, and it has become an enormous worldwide success. It is said that more than 15 million people in over 180 countries do Zumba regularly.

There are several different forms of Zumba. These can be very easy to do or very strenuous indeed! Because of this, almost anyone of any age can do Zumba. It's an excellent way to keep fit and lose weight. Zumba helps to make muscles stronger, to improve posture – and it's a great way to make new friends, too. And if you can't get to a class, there is, of course, an app that lets you take part in Zumba wherever you are.

3 CAPOEIRA

Another activity that mixes dance and exercise is capoeira. It is an Afro-Brazilian martial art that has become increasingly popular around the world. Capoeira was developed in Brazil in the 16th century. African slaves who had been brought to Brazil used it as a way to practise a martial art in secret. Because it is always performed to music, slave owners thought it was a dance.

To the steady rhythm of the music from a berimbau (a type of string instrument played with a bow), two people perform a series of kicks and flips, but without ever actually touching each other – at least, not intentionally! It is a demanding form of fitness activity that needs strength and balance and can be done by people of all ages.

2 10.06 **Read and listen to the article. Answer the questions.**

1 How long are ParkRun races and when do they happen?
2 What are the ParkRun events intended to do?
3 What two activities did Zumba bring together?
4 Why is it not absolutely necessary to go to a class to do Zumba?
5 Why was capoeira originally a secret activity?
6 How is capoeira a challenging exercise?

3 SPEAKING **Have you ever tried any of these activities? Would you like to? Why? Discuss with a partner.**

I haven't tried capoeira, but I would like to!

4 VOCABULARY There are eight highlighted words in the article. Match the words with these meanings. Write the words.

0 encouraging people to support something *promoting*
1 needing a lot of energy ______
2 meaning to ______
3 invented (a system, plan etc.) ______
4 a sport that is a form of defending yourself ______
5 not changing very much ______
6 the way in which someone stands or sits ______
7 needing a lot of physical effort ______

5 SPEAKING Discuss these questions with a partner.

- Which of the three activities would be the most popular at your school? Why?
- What other fun activities have you heard of? Can you do any of them at your school?
- What do you do to stay fit and healthy?
- What do you think you should do more of?
- Do you think it's important for schools to encourage young people to stay fit? Why?

WRITING

A story

1 INPUT Read Jessica's story. Then answer the questions.

1 Why weren't Jessica and her friends happy at lunchtime on the last day of their holiday?
2 Why do you think Robbie said they couldn't go up the mountain?
3 What do you think Jessica and her friends learned from the experience?

2 Which of the words in bold in the story are used to:

1 talk about the time when things happened?
2 talk about the order in which things happened?
3 make the story more interesting?

3 ANALYSE Read the story again and answer the questions.

1 Which past tenses does the writer use in the first paragraph and why?
2 The story has four paragraphs. Which of them …
– sets the scene? (who? where? when?)
– explains the problem?
– talks about a dramatic situation?
– tells us about the solution to the problem?

A BIG MISTAKE

Last year I was staying at a holiday camp with some friends. **On the last day**, we wanted to go up a mountain near the camp. But it was **already lunchtime**, and it had been raining **all morning**. So Robbie, our guide, said, 'Sorry, guys, the weather is just too bad. We can't go.' We had all been looking forward to this mountain trip for days.

At first, we were really disappointed. **Then** one of my friends had an idea. 'Why don't we go anyway?' he said. 'Robbie won't notice, and we'll be back before it gets dark'. **Five minutes later** we were ready to leave.

We made good progress. 'We'll be at the top of the mountain in an hour,' we thought. But then the weather changed. It became foggy, and the rain became much heavier. **Suddenly**, we realised that we had lost our way.

Luckily, I had my mobile phone on me. We phoned Robbie at the camp. He told us to stay where we were. When he found us, it was already dark. We were really sorry. We had made a big mistake.

4 PLAN Choose an activity and think of a real or imagined story. Make a plan that helps you to tell the story in four paragraphs. Make notes about ideas for each of them.

5 PRODUCE Write your story in about 200 words. Use Jessica's story to help you.

- Make sure your story is well structured.
- When you have finished, check the tenses you have used.
- Find a title that you think will make people want to read your story.

B1 Preliminary for Schools

READING

Part 3: 4-option multiple choice

→ workbook page 97

1 Read the text and questions below. For each question, choose the correct answer.

17-year-old Nadia Clarke talks about her African experience.

Last summer I got the chance to spend a month helping out in a hospital in Rwanda with my parents, who work for a charity. I had one year left at school, and I was interested in studying medicine at university. I thought it was the perfect chance to get some experience and to see if I really wanted to be a doctor.

It was a month that changed my life. I was introduced to a world that is very different to mine in so many ways, and I soon discovered how difficult people's lives can be. But I was also amazed at how positively people go about their everyday lives. The way they come together and help each other is a real inspiration, and something I think a lot of us here in the UK have forgotten. I think many of us don't realise how lucky we are.

My work in the hospital was hard. I spent a lot of time cleaning floors and changing bed sheets, but I also got to spend some time looking after the patients. And I got the chance to talk to some doctors and ask them about the profession. All of them told me how difficult being a doctor in that hospital was sometimes – hard work and long hours, and so many emotional challenges. But all of them also said that they didn't want to practise their profession anywhere else, because having seen the effect they were having on that community, they just wanted to go on. At times, it was a difficult experience, but it didn't change my mind about being a doctor. In fact, it only made me more determined to do medicine and to be like the doctors and nurses I worked with there.

When I finish, I know exactly what I'm going to do: I want to work for an international organisation like the Red Cross or Médecins sans Frontières, so I can spend my life helping people overseas who really need it. I can't wait to get started.

1 Why did Nadia want to go to Rwanda with her parents?
- A She wanted to learn more about being a doctor before deciding on what to study at university.
- B She wanted to help her parents and work for a charity in Rwanda.
- C She wanted to go on a month-long holiday with her parents before going to university.
- D She wanted to make an important decision about her final year at school.

2 What surprised Nadia the most about the experience?
- A She missed the UK more than she imagined and wanted to go home.
- B She was surprised at the kindness and attitude of the people despite the daily challenges.
- C There was no difference in her opinion before or after the experience.
- D She found it difficult to understand the differences between life in Rwanda and her own life.

3 What did the doctors Nadia worked with tell her?
- A They did not want to be doctors anywhere else.
- B It was hard work and long hours, with little satisfaction.
- C They hoped to go on to work in other communities and have a similar effect.
- D They liked the positive and negative feelings that they experienced while working in the hospital.

4 In paragraph 4, Nadia mentions that …
- A she would prefer to have a job as a doctor in her hometown.
- B she doesn't think helping people is a good career choice.
- C she is still thinking about working for a charity like her parents.
- D she is completely sure of her future professional career plans.

5 What might Nadia write home to her friends?
- A The doctors have been really kind here, but I'm not so sure it's what I want to do anymore.
- B The people are very friendly, and I've made some really good friends.
- C It's been difficult, but I really want to work somewhere like this when I'm older.
- D Sweeping floors and cleaning beds! I want to spend more time with the patients.

LISTENING

Part 3: Gap fill

→ workbook page 53

2 10.07 **You will hear a man talking about summer jobs at the local newspaper. For each question, write one or two words or a number or a date or a time.**

The Daily Post – Summer Jobs

The jobs are for people looking for experience in [1]______ .

The newspaper is looking for two [2]______ .

The weekly timetable is Mondays and [3]______ – 1 pm to 6 pm.

Job is for four weeks starting on [4]______ .

Application forms on the [5]______ or in the newspaper – this week only!

Contact [6]______ for more information.

TEST YOURSELF UNITS 9 & 10

VOCABULARY

1 Complete the sentences with the words in the list. There are two extra words.

as | as soon as | career | challenging | feel | in | make | notice | take | then | training | until

1 If you aren't sleeping very well, perhaps you should ____________________ more exercise.
2 My brother's working ____________________ a postman for the summer.
3 Have you ever thought about a ____________________ in marketing?
4 The job's OK, but it isn't very ____________________ , so sometimes I don't enjoy it much.
5 At the beginning, we got lots of on-the-job ____________________ so we could do it properly.
6 My mum used to be a teacher, but now she works ____________________ the travel industry.
7 He didn't like his job much, so after a month, he gave in his ____________________ .
8 I'm going to keep trying ____________________ I find the answer!
9 I don't feel well. I'm going to phone the doctor and ____________________ an appointment.
10 I'll call you ____________________ the train arrives. /10

GRAMMAR

2 Complete the sentences with the words in the list. You need to write the correct form of the verbs.

build (x2) | invite (x2) | work (x2)

1 After I left school, I ____________________ in a shop.
2 Our school ____________________ in 1965.
3 We ____________________ to a party next weekend, but I don't know if we can go.
4 My dad ____________________ at the school for 20 years when he left his job there.
5 Every year, my sister ____________________ to talk at a conference, and she always says yes.
6 They ____________________ their house in only six months!

3 Find and correct the mistake in each sentence.

1 Millions of hamburgers eat every day.
2 When we got to Moscow, we had being travelling for 12 hours.
3 Hundreds of buildings have damaged by the earthquake.
4 The boy was very ill, so they were taken him to hospital.
5 Last week, I hurt in a football match.
6 When he left college, he was a student there for four years. /12

FUNCTIONAL LANGUAGE

4 Complete the mini-dialogues with the words in the list.

about | afraid | better | feeling | hurts | see | sounds | together

1 A My leg ____________________ really badly.
B Oh, really? Perhaps you should go and ____________________ a doctor.
2 A Nadia, how ____________________ coming shopping with me on Saturday?
B Well, yes, that ____________________ fun. Thanks.
3 A I haven't been ____________________ well this morning.
B Oh, I'm sorry to hear that. I'm sure you'll feel ____________________ soon.
4 A I thought we could do something ____________________ tonight.
B I'm really sorry, but I'm ____________________ I can't. /8

MY SCORE /30

22–30 | 10–21 | 0–9

11 BREAKING NEWS

OBJECTIVES

FUNCTIONS: reporting what someone has said; expressing feelings: anger

GRAMMAR: reported statements; verb patterns: object + infinitive

VOCABULARY: fun; more verbs with object + infinitive; expressions with *make*

Get THINKING

▶31 Watch the video and think: would you want to be a journalist?

1

3

2

4

READING

1 Look at the photos. Do you follow the news? How? Do you use any of these sources?

2 SPEAKING Work in pairs. Think about the news on TV, in newspapers or on the internet. What should a news story be?

(0 – not important – 3 very important)

☐ truthful	☐ funny	☐ educational
☐ entertaining	☐ serious	☐ up-to-date

3 Think of stories you have heard recently for each of the categories in Exercise 2.

4 SPEAKING Discuss in pairs. How do you think the internet has changed the news? Give examples of how this can be good and how it can be bad.

5 11.01 Read and listen to the article. Match the photos with the stories. Write the dates of the stories under the photos.

6 Read the article again. Which story are these people talking about?

1 'I heard about that. They got a famous actor to read out the story.'

2 'How could she keep that secret for so long?'

3 'People probably believed him because of his profession.'

IT'S ALL FAKE NEWS

With the increase of fake news, it can be hard at times to know whether the news we read is true or not. What started as people spreading funny stories over the internet has become something much more serious. At its very worst, fake news is used to make up stories that try to change people's opinions. It is also used to cover or 'hide' uncomfortable stories that some people might not want to answer questions about. These days, fake news can make a big difference to the world. It is, perhaps, the most serious problem facing the world's media.

But fake news is nothing new. It has always been with us. In the past it wasn't such a big problem, though. People used it more for a bit of fun, as these famous examples show.

1 In 1917 two young cousins, Elsie Wright and Frances Griffiths, were having fun taking photos in the garden with Elsie's father's camera. When Mr Wright developed the photos, he saw that they showed the girls playing with fairies. The girls insisted the fairies were real. Elsie's father said he thought the girls were playing a joke on him, but Elsie's mother believed they were real. The photos were shown to the famous author of the Sherlock Holmes stories, Sir Arthur Conan Doyle, who also decided they were real. For years many people were fooled. The truth was only discovered in the 1980s when Elsie finally admitted that the fairies were just made out of paper.

2 For many years people thought that Loch Ness, a large lake in Scotland was home to a giant creature. In 1934, a doctor, Colonel Robert Wilson, announced that he had proof that it existed. He said that while he had been driving past the lake, he had seen the monster in the water. Luckily, he had had his camera with him and had been able to take some photos. The photo fooled many people until 1984, when it was proved to be fake.

3 On the day before Halloween, in 1938, many Americans were listening to the radio when suddenly the programme was interrupted. The announcer said that aliens had invaded the world. Lots of people started to panic. They left their homes and they were going to look for somewhere safe to hide. In fact, what they had heard was the beginning of a radio play of a famous novel by HG Wells, *War of the Worlds*, which is all about an alien invasion.

A ______

B ______

C ______

THINK values

Reacting to jokes

7 SPEAKING **Look at the reactions of four people who believed the Loch Ness story and then found out it was just a joke. In pairs, discuss each reaction. Whose reaction do you like most? Why?**

1 'How could I believe that? I feel really stupid and embarrassed.'
2 'It's a really great story. I think it's funny that I believed it.'
3 'It is funny, but I do feel a bit silly for believing it.'
4 'Why would someone want to play such a stupid joke? It makes me angry.'

Number 1 is too serious. It was just a silly joke. It's not important …

8 SPEAKING **Work in pairs. Think of a time when you were the target of a joke. How did you feel? Do you feel differently about it now?**

I remember once my friend …
At the time I felt / I didn't think …
Now I …

9 SPEAKING **Discuss these questions in small groups.**

1 Think of a time when a joke went wrong. What was it and why did it go wrong?
2 Why do you need to be careful when thinking about playing a joke?

GRAMMAR
Reported statements

1 Look at the article on page 103 again. How are these statements reported? Write down how the underlined words change.

0 I think the girls are playing a joke on me.
thought were playing
1 I believe the fairies are real.
______
2 The fairies are just made out of paper.
______
3 While I was driving past the lake, I saw the monster in the water.
______
4 Aliens have invaded the world.
______
5 They are going to look for somewhere safe to hide.
______

2 Use the example sentences in Exercise 1 to complete the rules.

RULE: When we report what people say, we often change the verb tenses:
- present simple → 1 *past simple*
- present continuous → 2 ______
- past simple → 3 ______
- past continuous → 4 ______
- present perfect → 5 ______
- *am/is/are going to* → 6 ______
- *can/can't* → 7 ______
- *will/won't* → 8 ______

We often use the verbs *say* and *tell* to report.
After *tell*, use an object (*me, her, them*, etc.). After *say*, don't use an object.

3 Complete the sentences with the correct form of *say* or *tell*.

0 My dad *told* me that he wanted me to tidy my room.
1 The teacher ______ us that we could go home early.
2 I ______ that I was going to phone you when I got home.
3 The weatherman ______ that it would be sunny later.
4 She ______ him that she hadn't forgotten his birthday.
5 They ______ that they were visiting their grandparents on Saturday.
6 He ______ that he had left the books on the desk for me.
7 Dad ______ us we could stay at the party until eleven.
8 He ______ that someone was following him, but I ______ him he was imagining it.

4 Rewrite these quotes as reported speech.

0 'I work really hard.' (He said ...)
He said that he worked really hard.
1 'I flew back from Africa on Friday.' (She told ...)
2 'We've met lots of interesting people.' (They said ...)
3 'I'm going to write a book one day.' (He told ...)
4 'I can work for two days without sleeping.' (You said ...)
5 'We'll call you from the airport.' (They told me ...)
6 'I'm working on a really interesting story.' (She said ...)
7 'I need a holiday.' (He told ...)
8 'I was writing in my diary when your text arrived.' (She told him ...)

→ workbook page 100

VOCABULARY
Fun

5 Read the sentences and think of a sentence to follow each one to explain the meaning of the word in italics.

1 The English summer course was *fun*. ☐
2 I love Steve. He's *hilarious*. ☐
3 Why is everyone *laughing at* me? ☐
4 I don't *get* that *joke*. ☐
5 We *played* a *joke* on him. ☐
6 I'm rubbish at *telling jokes*. ☐
7 I'm not sure she liked you *making fun* of her. ☐
8 That's not *funny* at all. ☐

6 Match sentences a–h with sentences 1–8 from Exercise 5.

a Did I say something silly?
b I always forget the endings.
c She seems quite upset.
d I made loads of new friends there.
e Please don't do it again.
f I mean he's really, really funny.
g But I'm not sure he thought it was funny.
h Can someone explain it to me?

7 SPEAKING Discuss these questions in pairs.

1 Who's the funniest person you know?
2 Are you good at telling jokes? Why or why not?
3 Do you always get jokes? What do you do when you don't understand?
4 Have you ever played a good joke on someone? What was it?
5 What's the funniest thing you have ever done?

→ workbook page 102

WRITING
A news report

8 **Choose one of the headlines below and write a short news report for it. Try to include two examples of reported speech.**

FOUND – THE WORLD'S FUNNIEST JOKE

GOOD JOKE GOES WRONG

LISTENING

9 **Which of these words do you associate with the extreme weather conditions in the photos?**

ice | rain | snow | wind

1

tornado

2

blizzard

3

flood

4

hailstorm

10 11.02 **Warren Faidley is an extreme weather journalist. Listen and say the types of weather in Exercise 9 that he reports on. Then answer the question.**

What is the difference between a weatherman and a weather journalist?

11 11.02 **Listen again. For each question, choose the correct answer.**

1 How did he escape from the river when he was 12?

A B C

2 What danger did he escape from with his father when he was a child?

A B C

3 Which of these photos gave Faidley his lucky break?

A B C

4 Which of these is the charity that Faidley has started?

A B C

WordWise: Expressions with *make*

12 **Complete the expressions from the unit so far with a word from the list.**

angry | difference | friends | fun | up

1 Fake news is used to make ______ stories that try to change what we believe.
2 These days fake news can make a big ______ to the world.
3 Why would someone want to play such a stupid joke? It makes me ______ .
4 I'm not sure she liked you making ______ of her.
5 I made loads of new ______ there.

13 **Complete the sentences with *make* + another word.**

1 Doing a lot of exercise can ______ a ______ to your health.
2 When you move to a new school, it can be difficult to ____________________ with people.
3 It isn't very nice to ____________________ of other people.
4 Is that story really true? Or did you ______ it ______ ?
5 Those newspaper stories are not accurate. They really ______ me ______ .

→ workbook page 102

READING

1 **Imagine you are going to be interviewed by a journalist on a TV programme about a subject you know a lot about. Read and answer the questions. Make notes.**

1 What is your specialist subject?
Arsenal

2 What do you know about it?
all the players, the history of the club

2 SPEAKING **Work in pairs. Tell your partner about your specialist subject and what you can say about it.**

My specialist subject is Arsenal. I can tell you about all the players. I can tell you where they are from, how old they are ...

3 11.03 **Read and listen to the article. Match the people with the descriptions.**

1 ☐ Robert E Kelly — a an expert
2 ☐ James Menendez — b a wife
3 ☐ Jung-a Kim — c a journalist

4 **Read the article again. Put the events in the order they happened. Write 1–9 in the boxes.**

☐ The interviewer mentions the professor's child.
☐ Professor Kelly's daughter comes into the room.
☐ Professor Kelly's baby son comes into the room.
☐ Professor Kelly says sorry for the interruption.
☐ The professor's wife closes the door.
☐ Professor Kelly tries to keep his daughter away from the camera.
☐ The interviewer asks Professor Kelly a question about Korean politics.
☐ Professor Kelly tries to keep calm and answer the question.
☐ The professor's wife comes into the room.

THE DANGER OF LIVE TV

Live interviews can be a dangerous thing. Over the years, many live news reports have been interrupted by people who want to get their faces on TV. Sometimes the journalists stop their reports and tell the people to go away, but most of the time they just carry on professionally and pay no attention to what's happening behind them.

As technology gets better, more and more TV interviews are done using communication software such as Skype©. An interviewer in the TV studio can interview someone who is sitting at their computer in their own home. It's a lot safer, you might think. Problems are rare and the interviews often go well. But things don't always go quite as planned. Just ask Professor Robert E. Kelly, an American politics professor at a South Korean university.

One day, Professor Kelly was being interviewed live on the BBC. He was speaking from his home in Busan, South Korea, where he had set up his computer in his home office.

The interviewer, James Menendez, was asking him to explain recent political events in the region. Suddenly the door behind him opened and Dr Kelly's young daughter, Marion, came in and danced her way over to her father. The interviewer mentioned that they had been joined by one of the professor's children, and as Dr Kelly put his arm out to try and stop his daughter from coming any closer, they were joined by another of his children. This time it was his baby son, James, who entered the room in a baby walker and rolled across the floor behind the professor. Dr Kelly tried to keep calm and carry on talking. He wanted his children to leave the room, but he couldn't stop the interview. Seconds later, Dr Kelly's wife, Jung-a Kim, came running into the room to his rescue. She grabbed one child in each hand and dragged them out of the room while the professor continued to offer his apologies. Finally, his wife reappeared on her hands and knees – trying to avoid being seen by the webcamera – to close the door behind her. Very embarrassed, Dr Kelly apologised and the interview continued.

Of course, this 40 seconds of live action was soon uploaded on to the internet and watched by millions all over the world, and immediately the professor, his wife and children became very famous. Indeed, the next time Professor Kelly was on the BBC, they wanted to interview Jung-a Kim, Marion and James, too.

Grammar rap! ▶32

GRAMMAR

Verb patterns: object + infinitive

5 **Put the words in order to make sentences from the text. Then complete the rule.**

1 tell / the / away / people / the journalists / to / go
2 asking / was / him / recent political / explain / the interviewer / events / to
3 the / he / leave / his / children / to / wanted / room

> **RULE:** Some verbs (*ask, want, tell*) are followed by an object (noun or personal [4]______) and the [5]______ form of the verb.
> *Mum asked me to tidy my room.*

6 **Look at pictures 1–4. What does the teacher ask the students to do? Write sentences.**

1

2

3

4

1 *Can you hand out the books, please?*
2 ______
3 ______
4 ______

7 **Work in pairs. Take turns to report the sentences in Exercise 6. Use *tell* and *ask*.**

He asked her to hand out the books.

→ workbook page 101

VOCABULARY

More verbs with object + infinitive

8 **Read what the people say. Match each one with a verb from the list.**

allow | encourage | ~~expect~~ | invite
persuade | remind | want | warn

0 'We think you should spend more time on your homework.' *expect*
1 'Slow down. You're going to crash.' ______
2 'Don't forget to watch the programme.' ______
3 'OK, you can go to the party.' ______
4 'You should definitely enter the talent show. You're a really good singer.' ______
5 'Take me to the Ed Sheeran concert – please. I'll be really good. I promise. You will? Oh, thank you!' ______
6 'I've chosen you to play in the school tennis team.' ______
7 'Would you like to go to the cinema?' ______

9 **Rewrite the sentences in Exercise 8 with the verbs you matched to each one.**

They expected me to spend more time on my homework.

→ workbook page 102

SPEAKING

10 **Think about these things. Make notes about them.**

1 Two things your parents allow you to do.
2 Two things your parents expect you to do.
3 Two things your parents warn you not to do.

11 **Work in pairs. Talk about your notes from Exercise 10.**

12 **Now discuss these things with your partner.**

1 Two things you expect your parents to do for you.
2 Two things you don't expect your parents to do for you any more.
3 Two things you expect your parents to do your whole life – even if you don't want them to.

PRONUNCIATION
Intonation: rude or polite? Go to page 121.

DEVELOPING SPEAKING

1 11.06 **Look at the photo. What do you think they are looking at? Listen and read to check.**

Tony: Hey, Sandra. Check this out. It's a tweet from Sam Johnson, and it's about your brother, Mark.

Sandra: Really? Let me see. 'Our match against Charlton school yesterday finished 1–1. We didn't win because Mark Smith missed an easy goal. Don't even know why he's in the team.' What! That's unfair. And I know for a fact that Mark scored our only goal. I'm going to have a word with Sam.

Tony: No, don't do that. It's not worth it.

Sandra: But it makes me so angry! Sam can't just post whatever he wants to post. Look, he's over there. I'm going to talk to him. Hey, Sam.

Sam: What's up? Oh, I think I know. My tweet about your brother, I guess.

Sandra: Well, yes. Why did you write that? And why didn't you say that he actually scored a goal?

Sam: I can write what I want. And anyway, I don't think your brother's a good player.

Tony: But we're talking about being truthful. He scored the goal. I think that's probably more important than his miss.

Sam: I'm just saying he isn't a good footballer. That's the truth. Get over it.

Tony: And he walks away! Incredible.

Sandra: OK, I'm going to write a tweet now. Here we go. 'I'm really cross! Sam Johnson tweeted something completely untrue about my brother. I think it's because he's jealous.'

Tony: No, Sandra. Don't say you're angry. Just tell people what he said.

Sandra: You're right. I'll change it. 'I asked Sam Johnson why he tweeted something untrue and unfair about my brother. He was like, "It just came into my head and I wrote it." Any thoughts, guys? Let me know!'

Tony: That's it. Let's see what your friends think. Look – someone's already replied.

2 Read the dialogue again and answer the questions.

1 Why is Sandra upset about Sam's tweet?
2 What does Sam think about Mark?
3 What does Sandra want to say in her first tweet?
4 Why does she change her mind about what to write?

3 SPEAKING **Discuss the questions in pairs.**

1 Is Sandra right to be angry?
2 Is Sam's reason for his tweet a good reason?
3 Which of Sandra's tweets is best, and why?
4 Should people always be truthful in their messages?

Phrases for fluency

4 Find the underlined expressions in the dialogue and use them to complete the conversation.

A Hi, [1]____________________ ! It's my new basketball kit.
B Oh, nice. I wish I could play in the next match.
A Did you talk to Alex about it?
B Yes. But [2]____________________ , 'No way, you can't play and that's that.'
A Really? That's bad. Should I [3]____________________ with him?
B No, it's OK, thanks.
A [4]____________________ , he shouldn't treat people like that.
B Hmm, but [5]____________________ a guy who thinks he is better than everyone else.
A Well, you never know.
B [6]____________________ . He won't listen to you.

FUNCTIONS
Expressing feelings: anger

KEY LANGUAGE
I get so angry ... I hate it ...
It makes me really cross / angry ...

5 Complete the mini-dialogues using the phrases from the Key Language box. Use the correct form of the verbs.

1 **Jorge** What's wrong Emily?
Emily My sister has been reading my texts. It ________ when she does that!
2 **Haruto** ________ it when people don't listen to what I'm saying!
Ethan Me, too! It's so annoying.
3 **Lena** What's up, Isabel?
Isabel My mum said I can't go to the party tomorrow. I ________ when she told me, but now I feel bad.

6 Make a list of the top three things that make you angry. Write sentences using the phrases in Exercise 5.

I get so angry when my brother takes my things.

7 SPEAKING **Work in pairs. Tell each other about the things on your lists.**

LIFE COMPETENCIES

Being assertive is making sure you say clearly what you want or think but respect what other people think, too. Being passive or aggressive hurts either you or the people around you, but being assertive means you let people know what's important to you, which is more likely to have positive results for everyone.

1 ▶ 33 **Watch the video. What was the problem with the meal?**

2 ▶ 33 **Watch again and answer the questions.**

1 Who wanted to talk to the waiter?
2 Why was Kieran's sister embarrassed?
3 How did the waiter react?
4 What did Kieran learn from the experience?

3 **Read the following situations. Decide which answer is passive, which is aggressive and which is assertive.**

1 A classmate wants to copy your homework.
  a Say no, and, in front of the whole class, shout, 'Somebody's not clever enough to do the homework!'
  b Give the classmate your homework. They might say bad things about you if you don't.
  c Say no, and explain why you don't think it's right to let them copy your work.

2 Your best friend promises to call you but doesn't.
  a Feel hurt, but don't say anything about it.
  b Call your friend and say, 'You said you were going to call me. Is everything OK?'
  c Be angry with your friend without saying why and stop talking to them.

3 You are in class and you don't understand what the teacher has asked you to do.
  a Sit and wait to see what the others do.
  b Start talking to your friends.
  c Put your hand up and say, 'Sorry, I didn't understand. Can you please explain again?'

4 You need to ask permission from your parents to stay out late.
  a Just stay out late and tell your parents that you didn't see the time.
  b Don't ask. They never give you permission to do anything, so why ask?
  c Tell your parents what time the film you want to see finishes, and ask to go.

5 You're in a bookshop looking for a book you want, but you can't find it.
  a Say, 'I can't find anything here! I'm going to a better shop.'
  b Ask the shop assistant to help you find the book.
  c Look on all the shelves again. You don't want to ask for help and look silly.

Me and my world

4 SPEAKING **Work in pairs. Act out one of these situations three times – once being passive, once being aggressive and once being assertive.**

- You're working on a group project, but you are doing much more work than the other members of the group.
- You asked your parents to sign a permission form for a school trip, but they haven't signed it yet.
- You're leaving a shop and notice that you have paid twice for something.

5 SPEAKING **Act out your situation for another pair, but don't tell them if you are being passive, aggressive or assertive. After you finish, the other pair guesses which one you are acting.**

6 SPEAKING **Work in small groups. Talk about a situation in your life when you should have been more assertive.**

TIPS FOR BEING ASSERTIVE

- **Remember that having a different point of view doesn't mean you are right and the other person is wrong.**
- **Be honest and tell others how you feel or what you want.**
- **Look at the other person and speak in a normal voice.**

12 RULES AND REGULATIONS

OBJECTIVES

FUNCTIONS:
talking about permission; following and giving simple instructions

GRAMMAR:
be allowed to / let; third conditional

VOCABULARY:
discipline; consequences and reasons

Get THINKING

Watch the video and think:
what rules in life are the most important?

READING

1 **Look at this list. Put a tick (✓) if it's something you can do. Put a cross (✗) if it's something you can't do.**

- ☐ stay up late at weekends
- ☐ invite friends to your home
- ☐ watch any TV programme you want
- ☐ wear any clothes you want at home
- ☐ wear any clothes you want to school
- ☐ use your mobile phone at school
- ☐ listen to music in your bedroom
- ☐ hang out with your friends in town

2 **Now look at the photos. What are the rules like at your school about the things you can see?**

3 **What other things can you think of that you can or can't do at home or at school?**

4 SPEAKING **Discuss with a partner. Who has stricter rules in their life?**

5 **Look at the pictures with the article on the next page. In what way did these children have a hard life?**

6 12.01 **Read and listen to the article to check your ideas. Under each picture write *Greek*, *Aztec* or *both*.**

7 **Read the article again and complete the sentences. Use between one and three words.**

1 Ancient Greek parents had __________ to decide if they wanted to keep their babies.
2 Unwanted babies often became __________ .
3 Unlike Greek girls, Greek boys __________ .
4 At military school Greek boys often didn't have __________ to eat.
5 Aztec children who broke the rules received __________ .
6 Ancient Aztecs thought education __________ .
7 Aztec boys and girls __________ to the same school.
8 *Calmecac* schools were for children from __________ .

HARD TIMES TO BE A KID

'I'm not allowed to stay out late.'
'Why do I have to do my homework before I can watch TV?'
'My parents never let me go to parties.'
'Why is it just Mum and Dad who make the rules? Life's just not fair.'

Do these complaints sound familiar? Well, if you think your life is hard, you might like to think about kids in ancient times. For some of them, life was really hard.

If you were born in Ancient Greece, you weren't even thought to be a real person until you'd been alive for five days. That's right – for five days after you were born, your parents were allowed to get rid of you. If they decided they didn't want you, they'd just leave you outside somewhere to die. Of course, you might get lucky and someone else might pick you up, but then you'd spend the rest of your life as their slave. However, if your parents decided that they wanted you as part of the family, then there was a special ceremony to welcome you.

Only the boys were allowed to go to school. Greek girls stayed at home, where their mothers taught them skills like cooking and weaving – things that would help them find a husband.

At the age of seven, some boys were sent away to very strict military schools, where they were taught how to become soldiers. Life was pretty hard at these schools. For example, the kids were often hungry. The teachers didn't let them have much food – for a reason. They wanted the boys to learn how to survive for themselves by stealing food. But if they got caught, they were punished.

Aztec children in Mesoamerica also had a difficult life in ancient times. If they broke any rules, they could expect some pretty nasty punishments.

On the plus side, Aztecs really believed in the importance of schooling. In the home, children learned practical skills: fathers taught their sons how to fish and farm while mothers taught their daughters home-making skills. Girls and boys also went to school (although the adults didn't let them go to the same schools).

Kids went to schools called *telpochcalli*. They had lessons about history, religion and music. The boys also had lessons in how to fight. If the children were from a more important family, they went to a *calmecac*, where they learned how to read and write, too.

At both schools children had to be on their best behaviour. They knew all about the punishments for behaving badly, and life was hard enough anyway.

THINK values

The importance of rules

8 Read the statements 1–4 and say what type of rule they are.

1 You're not allowed to ride bikes on the pavements.
2 Our parents don't let us leave the dinner table before everyone has finished.
3 I make sure that I tidy my room every weekend.
4 You can't ask a question unless you put your hand up.

a a personal rule
b a family rule
c a school rule
d a rule of society

9 SPEAKING **Work in pairs. Think of more rules (at least one each) for the four types (personal, family, school, society). What is the punishment for breaking these rules?**

GRAMMAR
be allowed to / let

1 Look at the example sentences. Then complete the rules with *be allowed to* and *let*.

1 I'm not allowed to stay out late.
2 My parents never let me go to parties.
3 For five days after you were born, your parents were allowed to get rid of you.
4 The teachers didn't let them have much food.

> **RULE:** To talk about permission we can use ***be allowed to*** and ***let***.
> We use [5]______ when there's no need to identify who gives (or doesn't give) the permission. The subject of the sentence is the person who receives (or doesn't receive) the permission.
> Form this with subject + [6]______ (*not*) + ***allowed to*** + [7]______. It is a passive construction.
> We use [8]______ when the subject of the sentence is (or isn't) giving the permission.
> Form this with subject + [9]______ + [person] + verb.

2 Rewrite the sentence using the words in brackets.

0 My parents don't let me go out on school nights. (I / allowed)
I'm not allowed to go out on school nights.
1 I wasn't allowed to go to the party. (My parents / let)
2 My mum didn't let me walk to school on my own until I was 12. (I / allowed)
3 We aren't allowed to text in class. (The teacher / let)
4 My dad lets me play his electric guitar. (I / allowed)
5 My sister is allowed to stay up until 11 pm on Saturday nights. (Dad / let)

3 Choose three of the things in the list and write two true sentences and one false sentence about yourself.

- play video games every day for as long as I want
- watch TV before school
- use my mobile during dinner
- go to the cinema by myself
- buy my own clothes
- meet my friends on a school night

4 SPEAKING **Work in pairs. Read out your sentences. Can your partner guess which sentence isn't true?**

My parents let me go out on a school night.

That isn't true.

→ workbook page 108

VOCABULARY
Discipline

5 Match the phrases 1–6 with the definitions a–f.

1 to do what you're told ☐
2 to behave well ☐
3 to get punished ☐
4 to break the rules ☐
5 to get into trouble ☐
6 to get told off ☐

a to be good by acting in the correct way
b to do something you shouldn't do
c to have problems because you did something wrong
d to follow the rules that others make
e to be told that what you did was wrong
f to be made to do something you don't want to do because you did something wrong

6 Complete the sentences with phrases from Exercise 5. Sometimes there is more than one possible answer.

1 My sister Claire breaks all the school rules, so she always gets ______ .
2 Kenny always ______ in class. The teacher thinks he's perfect.
3 Ana doesn't often listen to her parents. Her mum and dad would be a lot happier if sometimes she ______ .
4 My little brother Stan is really naughty. He's always getting ______ .
5 Julia's a rebel. She likes ______ .
6 If I don't behave well, I usually get ______ .

7 Which of the children in Exercise 6 do you think these pictures show?

A ☐

B ☐

C ☐

8 SPEAKING **Which sentences are true for you? Compare with your partner.**

- I always do what I'm told.
- I often get told off by my parents and teachers.
- I'm always getting into trouble.
- I never break the rules. I think rules are important!
- I think people should get punished for bad behaviour.
- If you behave well all the time, it's boring!

→ workbook page 110

LISTENING

9 SPEAKING **What do you know about the game of chess? Discuss with a partner.**

10 12.02 **Listen to Lucia talking about chess and look at the chessboard. What are the different pieces called?**

11 12.02 **Listen again and answer the questions.**

1 What is the aim of the game?
2 What can pawns do on their first move?
3 What can the knights do that other pieces can't?
4 What happens if a king is in 'checkmate'?
5 Which colour starts the game?
6 What happens if the pawn reaches the other side of the board?

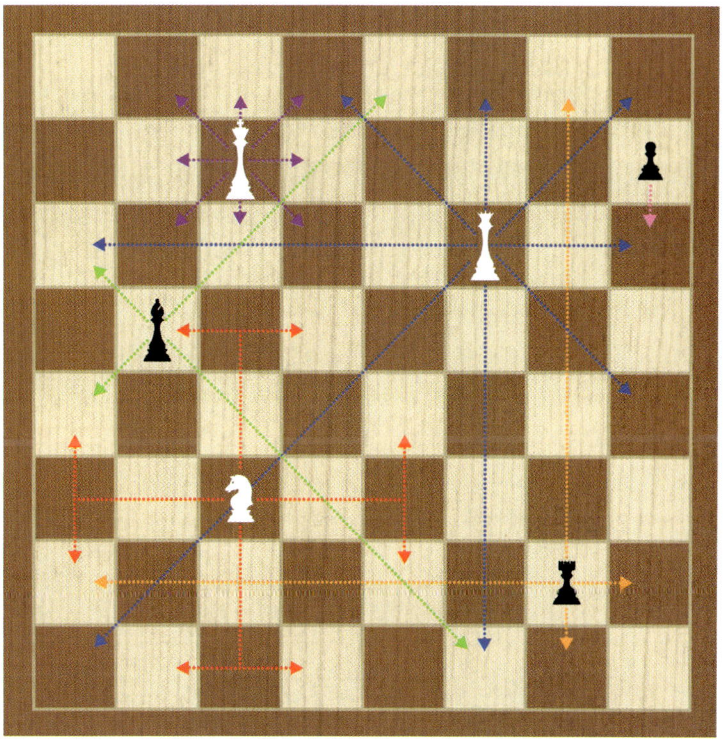

FUNCTIONS

Following and giving simple instructions

12 **Think of a simple game you like to play that needs two or more people. Answer the questions and make notes.**

- What do you need to play? Dice? Cards?
- How many players are needed to play the game?
- How do the players know when it is their turn to play?
- Do the players score points? If yes, how?
- What are the players *not* allowed to do?

13 SPEAKING **Work in pairs. Describe to each other how to play your game.**

Before you start, …	Then …
So how do you play/win?	Finally, …
The player who …	First …

Train to TH!NK

Being creative

14 **Look at the chess pieces. What do you think they could be called?**

I think number one could be a dragon.

15 **In pairs, talk about the pieces.**

1 What moves can they make?
2 What 'special' powers do they have?

16 **Now think of three different chess pieces. Make notes and design them. Think about what they look like and how they can move.**

17 SPEAKING **Show your pieces to your classmates and discuss your ideas.**

Mine moves around other pieces.

READING

1 12.03 Read and listen to the results of a contest carried out by a fiction-writing website. Match the pictures with the stories.

Home About Join in New stories

A

Small is beautiful. So every week we invite our readers to send us their (very) short stories. Each story must be exactly 50 words, not a word more, not a word less – just like this introduction. (Words like 'didn't' count as one word.) And then we publish all our favourites!

B

C

Here are the best from last week's topic:

Changing the Rules

1 'Want to play in the school football team?' the sign said. 'Come along at four o'clock!' So I went. 'But you're a girl!' a boy said. 'Girls can't play in the school team!' 'There's no rule,' I said. And I played. Now there's a rule – everyone can play in the school team.

2 It was the last biscuit. Both of us wanted it. 'Let's toss a coin,' my brother said. 'Heads I win, tails you lose.' He tossed the coin. 'Tails – you lose' and he ate the last biscuit. If I had listened to his rules more carefully, maybe the biscuit would have been mine.

3 I hate cabbage. When I was a small boy, my father made me eat it at lunch. 'The rule is: eat everything on your plate,' he said. I ate it and then I was sick. When I'm a father, my rule will be: 'If you don't like it, you can leave it.'

4 'They're my rules,' Kevin said. 'If you don't like them, find someone else to play with.' When he went to bed later that evening, Kevin felt sad. Playing ball on his own hadn't been much fun. If his rules hadn't been so unpopular, he wouldn't have spent the afternoon on his own.

5 In 1823, William Webb Ellis was playing football in his PE lesson. He picked up the ball and ran towards the goal. Everyone was shocked. 'You can't do that!' they shouted. 'I can,' he said as he put the ball in the goal. 'I've invented a new game. It's called rugby.'

D

E

2 **Match the stories (1–5) to the titles. Write the numbers. There is one title you don't need.**

- a No one wanted to play ☐
- b A long wait ☐
- c Game for all ☐
- d How a new sport was invented ☐
- e An unfair game ☐
- f Parents don't always know best ☐

3 **Each of the stories actually has 52 words. Find two words that you can take out in each one. (There may be more than one pair of words you can delete.)**

4 **Which of the stories are these people talking about? Do you agree with them?**

- a 'Children should always eat what they are given by their parents.' ☐
- b 'There shouldn't be different teams for boys and girls.' ☐
- c 'Things never change if you don't break the rules.' ☐
- d 'Brothers and sisters always try to trick each other.' ☐
- e 'It's important to be flexible when you make the rules.' ☐

5 WRITING **Choose one of the situations, make a rule for it and use it as a topic for your own 50-word short story.**

- Anyone who wants to come into my bedroom
- Using your phone at the dinner table
- Doing homework
- Taking food from the fridge
- Bedtime on a Friday night

GRAMMAR
Third conditional

6 **Read these sentences from the stories on page 114 and answer the questions. Then complete the rules.**

*If I **had listened** to his rules more carefully, maybe the biscuit **would have been** mine.*

1 Did she listen to her brother? Did she get the biscuit?

*If his rules **hadn't been** so unpopular, he **wouldn't have spent** the afternoon on his own.*

2 Were his rules popular? Did he spend the afternoon on his own?

RULE: To talk about unreal situations in the past and their imagined results, we use the third conditional.
- Condition clause: ***If*** + [3] ________ .
- Result clause: ***would*** (***not***) ***have*** + [4] ________ participle.

The condition clause can come before or after the result clause.

7 **Match the parts of the sentences.**

1 If I had studied harder, ☐
2 If I hadn't studied so much, ☐
3 Would she have been late for school ☐
4 If she hadn't got up when her alarm rang, ☐
5 If we hadn't spent all our money, ☐
6 We wouldn't have had enough money to go to the cinema ☐

a I wouldn't have passed the test.
b if she had got up when her alarm rang?
c we would have bought him a present.
d the test would have been a lot easier for me.
e if we had spent it all on food.
f she wouldn't have had time for breakfast.

8 **Put the verbs into the correct form to make third conditional sentences.**

0 If she *hadn't been* (not be) so rude, I *would have helped* (help) her.
1 If Paul ________________ (not invite) me to his party, I ________________ (be) really upset.
2 If she ________________ (enter) the competition, I'm sure she ________________ (win) it.
3 They ________________ (go) in the sea if they ________________ (not forget) their swimsuits.
4 We ________________ (not win) the game if he ________________ (not score) that goal.

9 **Read the statement. Imagine a different past and write as many third conditional sentences as you can. Compare your ideas with a partner.**

My grandparents met each other on holiday.

→ workbook page 109

VOCABULARY
Talking about consequences and reasons

10 **Match the conversations with the pictures. Write the numbers 1–4.**

1 A Why did you stop playing?
  B *Because* it started raining, Mum!
2 A So, your parents are angry with you again?
  B Yes. It's *because of* my bad marks at school.
3 A I was really hungry when I got home from school.
  B *That explains why* there aren't any biscuits left.
4 A I forgot to invite Jim to my party.
  B *So that's the reason* he looks so upset.

11 **Complete the sentences with your own ideas.**

1 A My football team lost again yesterday.
  B *That explains why …*
2 A I've just come back from a two-week holiday.
  B *That's why …*
3 A It's my best friend's birthday today.
  B *So that's the reason …*
4 A Is this your favourite computer game?
  B *That's right. It's because of …*

→ workbook page 110

PRONUNCIATION
Silent consonants Go to page 121.

TH!NK

Laws from around the world

Culture

1 Look at the pictures and answer the questions.

1 Each picture is about a strange law. What do you think the law is for each picture?

2 In one picture, someone is breaking a law. Can you guess which one?

A

2 🔊 12.06 Read and listen to the article to check your ideas from Exercise 1 and then do the quiz.

B

3 Read the laws again and mark the sentences T (true) or F (false).

1 You mustn't climb trees. ______

2 You can take a lion to the cinema but not any other wild animal. ______

3 It is free to tie an elephant to a parking meter. ______

4 Donkeys mustn't be put in a bathtub. ______

5 You mustn't go to the toilet after 10 pm. ______

6 Taxi drivers have to pay money to listen to music in their cars. ______

STRANGE laws from around the world

Laws are important – they help us to live together in a friendly, happy and **peaceful** way. However, there are a number of laws from various countries around the world that seem really strange. Many of them are rather old, but have never been changed. We've selected some of the strangest for you here.

1 It is against the law to **jump the queue** in the ticket hall in the underground metro system in ______ .

A New York, US **B** Paris, France **C** London, UK

2 If you climb a tree in ______ , you are **breaking the law**.

A Beijing, China **B** Oshawa, Canada **C** Tokyo, Japan

3 You can't take a pet lion to the cinema in ______ – if you have one!

A Amsterdam, the Netherlands **B** Baltimore, US **C** Madrid, Spain

4 If you don't walk your dog at least three times a day in ______ , you will get a **fine**.

A Turin, Italy **B** Berlin, Germany **C** Geneva, Switzerland

5 If you tie an elephant to a parking meter in ______ , you have to pay a parking **fee**.

A Amsterdam, the Netherlands **B** Madrid, Spain **C** Florida, US

6 If you go to the toilet at night in ______ , you must remember that it is **illegal** to flush the toilet after 10 pm.

A Thailand **B** The Netherlands **C** Switzerland

7 If you are a taxi driver in ______ , and you play the radio while driving a customer, you have to pay **royalties** to the musicians you listen to during the journey.

A Italy **B** Greece **C** Finland

8 If you **own** a donkey in ______ , you must not keep it in the bathtub.

A Georgia, US **B** Istanbul, Turkey **C** London, UK

C

D

4 SPEAKING Which of the laws do you think is the strangest? Compare with others in the class.

5 VOCABULARY There are eight highlighted words in the article. Match the words with these meanings. Write the words.

1 doing something that is not allowed ____________
2 money you pay to allow you to do something ____________
3 have something that is yours ____________
4 money given to the writer of a song each time it is played ____________
5 move in front of people who were there before you ____________
6 money you pay for doing something wrong ____________
7 against the law ____________
8 without violence ____________

WRITING
A set of rules

1 INPUT Jemma wrote a set of rules for her house and her family for weekends. What does she say about:

1 food?	5 her sister?
2 sleep?	6 school and teachers?
3 her room?	7 TV?
4 homework?	8 herself?

2 Put the words in the correct order to make sentences from Jemma's rules. What do the sentences tell you about how she feels about homework, her sister and football?

1 allowed / ask / no one / me / is / homework / about / to

____

2 all / isn't / she / at / room / come / allowed / into / to / my

____

3 watch / no one / programme / time / at / other / can / any / that

____

3 ANALYSE Find the phrases and sentences in Jemma's rules that show she isn't 100% serious.

4 PLAN Choose one of the sets of rules below to write about. Make notes about what you want to include in the rules. (You don't have to be serious, but don't be unkind!)

- A set of rules for your family for the weekend.
- A set of rules for your family for the school holidays.
- A set of rules for you and your family when you go out together (e.g. to the cinema or to a restaurant).
- A set of rules for you and your family when you go somewhere on holiday together.
- A set of rules for … anything you like!

Rules for the weekend at home

1. After school finishes on Friday, Mum and Dad are not allowed to talk to me about school or teachers.
2. Between seven o'clock on Friday evening and nine o'clock on Sunday evening, no one is allowed to ask me about homework. (At other times, they can help me if they want.)
3. No noise before 10 am on Saturday. Saturday is my morning for sleeping.
4. For breakfast on Sunday, I can eat anything I want. Anything at all!!! (And that includes ice-cream!)
5. My sister Juliana is not allowed to use my computer – in fact, she isn't allowed to come into my room at all. (Well, only if she brings chocolate.)
6. My room – I will tidy it late on Sunday, but before then: keep out!
7. If there is a football match on TV with my team, no one can watch any other programme at that time.
8. And lastly – I am not allowed to be boring about rules 1–7!

JEMMA (the boss!)

5 PRODUCE Write the set of rules you chose in Exercise 4. Write about 150–180 words. Give them a title. Add some drawings if you want to.

B1 Preliminary for Schools

READING

Part 4: Gapped text

→ workbook page 25

1 Five sentences have been removed from the text below. For each question, choose the correct answer. There are three extra sentences which you do not need to use.

An exhibition at the Science Museum

It was fantastic to go to the Science Museum to see an exhibition about driverless vehicles.

Before my visit to the museum, I didn't know much about vehicles that drive themselves using computer controls. [1]______ . One way the exhibition did this was that it pushed me to ask questions about how much control we should let driverless cars have.

Driverless cars might seem like something from science fiction, but they've been around longer than we think. [2]______ . It was a car called the Citroen DS19, which was around back in 1960. It drove itself by following a network of cables buried underground. Driverless vehicles have developed a lot since then. Newer ones are used for different purposes, like helping farmers by picking crops, or scientists by exploring under the ice in the Arctic Ocean.

The exhibition was organised into three different zones. [3]______ . The first was called 'Land'. I was able to look at how driverless vehicles are already being used on land, and possible developments that will happen in the future.

The issue of safety is a big one. How can a driverless car make the choices a human makes? [4]______ . I understood more about how difficult it is when I was playing with the interactive displays. Doing this lets you see the world through the 'eyes' of a driverless car. It's very hard to program a computer to make the decisions a driver usually makes.

In the zone called 'Air', I learned about the flying drones that are being developed to deliver products, but not just for shoppers. [5]______ . And in the final zone, 'Water', driverless vehicles are being used to make maps of the sea floor and to understand how climate change is affecting the oceans. The whole exhibition was incredibly interesting and made a great day out!

- **a** Despite this, the vehicles used to be more popular.
- **b** I learned that the first of them appeared years ago.
- **c** If the technology improved, there'd be more like that.
- **d** They're also important for things like medical emergencies.
- **e** In fact, I wish I knew more about how it's made.
- **f** Scientists are working on ways to solve this problem.
- **g** Nor had I thought about them, so going there challenged me.
- **h** Each one of these sections dealt with a different subject.

LISTENING

Part 4: Multiple choice

→ workbook page 89

2 12.07 **You will hear a girl called Lucy talking on a TV programme about a competition she won. For each question, choose the correct answer.**

1 To enter the competition, Lucy had to
- **A** upload a video of herself and then phone someone.
- **B** write to the studio and record a video.
- **C** explain why she wanted to win in a letter and send it with a video of herself.

2 How did Lucy find out that she was the winner of the competition?
- **A** They called her into the studio and told her.
- **B** She got a letter in the post.
- **C** The TV company phoned her.

3 Why did Lucy read the weather multiple times?
- **A** She was enjoying it.
- **B** To become familiar with the equipment.
- **C** She was making mistakes.

4 How did Lucy feel when she did the forecast?
- **A** very nervous
- **B** very worried
- **C** very excited

5 What was the weather like in the forecast Lucy gave?
- **A** There was a variety of types of weather.
- **B** The weather was mainly the same across the country.
- **C** Some areas had unusually freezing cold weather.

6 How have Lucy's future plans changed?
- **A** She'd like to be on TV.
- **B** She'd like to be a weather presenter.
- **C** She'd like to be a teacher.

VOCABULARY

1 Complete the sentences with the words in the list. There are two extra words.

because | because of | behaved | encouraged | expected
explains | fun | funny | reason | told | trouble | warned

1 I broke a plate and I got ______________ off by my parents.
2 We couldn't go out ______________ it was snowing.
3 I really didn't like that joke – it just wasn't ______________ .
4 I didn't want to do karate lessons, but my parents ______________ me to give them a try, so I did.
5 Oh, your alarm clock didn't ring. That ______________ why you were late.
6 I'm not surprised you feel ill. I ______________ you not to eat that old cheese!
7 He has lots of problems at school, and he's always getting into ______________ .
8 I was surprised when England won. I ______________ them to lose.
9 It rained almost the whole time, so our walk really wasn't a lot of ______________ .
10 We couldn't hear the teacher ______________ the noise outside.

/10

GRAMMAR

2 Complete the sentences with the words in the list. You need to write the correct form of the verbs.

allow | go (x2) | let | not eat (x2)

1 I ______________ to the concert if I'd had a ticket.
2 We wanted to go, but my mum didn't ______________ us.
3 He would have been OK if he ______________ a second cheeseburger.
4 When I was a little girl, I wasn't ______________ to watch TV after nine o'clock.
5 If I'd known there was meat in it, I ______________ it.
6 If everyone ______________ to the party, we'd have had a lot more fun.

3 Find and correct the mistake in each sentence.

1 They said me to stay at home.
2 Why didn't they let me to go out?
3 They wanted me answer some questions.
4 I reminded her to giving me back my magazine.
5 If I would have known, I wouldn't have told anyone.
6 They hadn't won the game if Matt hadn't played.

/12

FUNCTIONAL LANGUAGE

4 Complete the mini-dialogues with the words in the list.

allowed | because | hate | have | let | makes | reason | why

1 A I don't understand. Why won't you ______________ me read my book?
B ______________ it's nearly midnight, and you have to go to sleep!
2 A It ______________ me really angry when people don't tell the truth.
B I see. So that explains ______________ you were cross with Jim.
3 A We aren't ______________ to take our mobile phones into class.
B Oh. So that's the ______________ why you didn't phone me.
4 A I ______________ it when people shout at me. It's horrible!
B Well, I wouldn't ______________ shouted if you had listened to me the first time!

/8

MY SCORE /30

22–30 | 10–21 | 0–9

PRONUNCIATION

UNIT 1
Intonation and sentence stress

1 1.06 **Read and listen to the dialogue.**

Henry I know … let's learn to surf!
Lucy That's a great idea!
Henry Do you think so?
Lucy Of course! We'll need lessons.
Henry I'll phone the surf shop!
Lucy It'll be fun … we should definitely do it!

2 **Which words show that Lucy likes Henry's idea?**

3 1.07 **Listen and repeat the dialogue.**

UNIT 2
Word stress

1 2.05 **Read and listen to the dialogue.**

Sadie Jake, I can't believe it! Do you recognise that man over there?
Jake I suppose it could be someone we know …
Sadie How could you forget? Think, Jake!
Jake Oh, yeah! Now I remember! He's on that TV quiz show.
Sadie That's right. It's called 'Concentrate'. I wonder what he's doing here?

2 **How many syllables do the blue / red / green words have? Say these verbs and stress the correct syllable.**

3 2.06 **Listen and repeat the dialogue.**

UNIT 3
Words ending in /ə/

1 3.02 **Read and listen to the dialogue.**

Joe Why don't we go to the cinema? We can see *The Monster in the Computer*. Tammy Baker plays the monster.
Tess Well … there's also *River Adventure*. Tom Webster's a doctor in it.
Joe I know he's a better actor than Tammy Baker but *River Adventure* is a lot longer. If we see the shorter film, we can have dinner after.
Tess OK – it looks much funnier, too. And let's go to the Super Burger for dinner!

2 **Say the words ending in the short /ə/ sound.**

3 3.03 **Listen and repeat the dialogue.**

UNIT 4
The short /ʌ/ vowel sound

1 4.05 **Read and listen to the poem.**

My little cousin from London's coming on Monday.
She's young and lovely – and very funny.
She loves the sun and running and jumping.
She doesn't like studying or spending money.

2 **Say the words with the /ʌ/ vowel sound in blue.**

3 4.06 **Listen and repeat the poem.**

UNIT 5
been: strong /biːn/ and weak /bɪn/

1 5.03 **Read and listen to the dialogue.**

Jill Where have you been? The party's already started.
Pete Shh! I've been hiding in the kitchen.
Jill We've been looking for you everywhere. We want to play a game.
Pete Well, I've been trying to find a bin to put this sandwich in. It's horrible!

2 **Say the strong and weak forms of *been*, /biːn/ and /bɪn/. What other word sounds like /bɪn/?**

3 5.04 **Listen and repeat the dialogue.**

UNIT 6
/f/, /v/ and /b/ consonant sounds

1 6.07 **Read and listen to the advertisement.**

Visit the beautiful village of Victoria!
The village is surrounded by forests and farms.
There's a fantastic river for fishing.
You can buy souvenirs and see very old buildings.
There are buses to the beach from Monday to Friday.
You'll never forget your visit to Victoria!

2 **Say the words with the /f/, /v/ and /b/ sounds.**

3 6.08 **Listen and repeat the sentences.**

UNIT 7
Intonation of question tags

1 7.04 **Read and listen to the dialogue.**

Sam You do want to come, *don't you?*
Max I'm not sure. Jane's got those big dogs, *hasn't she?*
Sam Yes, they're enormous! But they're very friendly.
Max Well, I don't like dogs, *do I?*
Sam You're not afraid, *are you?*
Max Of course not!

2 **Look at the blue question tags. Choose the correct words in each sentence.**

Sam *knows* / *doesn't know* the answer to her questions. Her voice goes *up* / *down*.

Now look at the red question tags. Choose the correct words in each sentence.

Max *knows* / *doesn't know* the answer to his questions. His voice goes *up* / *down*.

3 7.05 **Listen and repeat the dialogue.**

UNIT 8
The /juː/ sound

1 8.03 **Read and listen to the dialogue.**

Teacher Hello, Stewart! How are you? You used to be one of my best students!
Stewart Hello, Mrs Jones. I'm studying music and computing at university now.
Teacher Music and computing! Isn't that an unusual combination?
Stewart Not really. In the future I'd like to write music programs for computers. It's really new technology and very exciting.

2 **Say the words with the /juː/ sound.**

3 8.04 **Listen and repeat the dialogue.**

UNIT 9
/tʃ/ and /dʒ/ consonant sounds

1 9.02 **Read and listen to the dialogue.**

Charlie If I could be anything, I'd choose to be a journalist. What about you, Jane?
Jane Journalism's a very dangerous job, Charlie. I'm going to be a chess player.
Charlie You've changed your mind! You wanted to be a Geography teacher.
Jane Yes. I've just joined a chess club. My coach thinks I've got a good chance of becoming a champion.

2 **Say the words with the /tʃ/ and /dʒ/ sounds.**

3 9.03 **Listen and repeat the dialogue.**

UNIT 10
/tʃ/ and /ʃ/ consonant sounds

1 10.04 **Read and listen to the dialogue.**

Pat Welcome back to the show. We're in the kitchen today with our chef, Mitchell.
Mitchell Hello. In this demonstration I'm making a special Russian dish.
Pat Watch carefully everyone, as our chef Mitchell makes the dish you see in this picture.
Mitchell Patricia, please put the oven at the right temperature while I chop the cherries … now we add the sugar – but you shouldn't use too much! And now it's ready to bake.
Pat And here's a finished one! It tastes delicious!

2 **Say the words with the /ʃ/ and /tʃ/ sounds.**

3 10.05 **Listen and repeat the dialogue.**

UNIT 11
Intonation: rude or polite?

1 11.04 **Read and listen to the dialogue.**

Clerk Could you put your bag down over there, please.
Mr Young Excuse me. Could you repeat that?
Clerk Yes, could you put that bag down over there!
Mr Young I mean, could you repeat that *politely*?
Clerk I'm *terribly* sorry. Could you put your bag down over there, please?

2 **Which sentences sound rude? Which polite?**

3 11.05 **Listen and repeat the dialogue.**

UNIT 12
Silent consonants

1 12.04 **Read and listen to the dialogue.**

Guard 1 Shh! Listen! Someone's talking in the next room.
Guard 2 Yes, and at this hour the castle should be empty.
Guard 1 We should investigate. Or, erm, should we write a report?
Guard 2 I can't answer that. All I know is that we mustn't stay here another minute!

2 **Say the words with the silent consonants in blue.**

3 12.05 **Listen and repeat the dialogue.**

GET IT RIGHT!

UNIT 1

Present perfect vs. past simple

Learners often use the present perfect when the past simple is required.

We use the past simple to talk about events which have taken place at a specific time. We use the present perfect to talk about events where the time is not specified.

✓ *I **went** on holiday with my family last year.*

✗ *I ~~have been~~ on holiday with my family last year.*

Write positive answers to the following questions using the words given in the correct tense.

0 Have you started your new job? (last weekend)
Yes, I have. I started my new job last weekend.

1 Have you seen the latest episode? (yesterday)

2 Have you been to France before? (two times)

3 Have you visited your grandparents recently? (a few days ago)

4 Have you seen John? (five minutes ago)

5 Have you changed your phone? (for a better one)

6 Have you earned any money recently? (over £100 last week)

UNIT 2

Present perfect with *for* or *since*

Learners often use the present simple with *for* or *since* when the present perfect is required.

We use the present perfect tense with both *for* and *since* referring to an earlier time which is still relevant now.

✓ ***I have known** him for three months.*

✗ *I ~~know~~ him for three months.*

Make new sentences in the perfect tense using the information given.

0 I started playing the guitar when I was six years old. I still play the guitar now.
I've played the guitar since I was six years old.

1 We were friends when we were ten. We are still friends now.

2 I saw her when I was five. I did not see her after that.

3 I started working in the newsagent's two years ago. I work there now.

4 You moved to Madrid six months ago.

5 My family travelled abroad in 2014. They did not travel abroad after that.

6 I changed schools last school year.

UNIT 3

Comparatives and *than*

Learners often use the wrong forms of adjectives, trying to use *more* where it is not possible, especially with *bigger* and *cheaper*.

For adjectives with one syllable, we add *-er* for the comparative.

✓ *In ten years' time my town will be **bigger** than now.*

✗ *In ten years' time my town will be ~~more big~~ than now.*

For adjectives with two syllables ending in *-y*, we make the comparative by adding *-ier*.

✓ *I find English **easier** than French.*

✗ *I find English ~~more easy~~ than French.*

Learners sometimes use *that* instead of *than*.

✓ *Sports clubs are much better **than** the gym.*

✗ *Sports clubs are much better ~~that~~ the gym.*

Correct the following sentences.

1 I am much more happy than before.

2 If you go to Europe, the weather will be better in July that in February.

3 Which is more old, football or rugby?

4 The beaches are cleaner in the countryside that in the city.

5 It will make you fitter and more healthy.

UNIT 4

Any vs. – (no article)

Learners often miss out *any* where it is needed in questions and negative statements.

✓ *Do you have **any** questions? If so, please visit me in my office.*

✗ *Do you have —— questions? If so, please visit me in my office.*

Choose the correct answer, *any* or – (no article).

1 In the countryside there aren't *any* / – discos.
2 I didn't take *any* / – notice of it and deleted it again.
3 I have been doing *any* / – homework.
4 We need *any* / – time to work on this.
5 I have been here for four months and I can't live here *any* / – longer.
6 Do you have *any* / – money I can borrow?

will vs. should

Learners sometimes use *will* instead of *should*.
We use *should* to give advice to someone, or to mean that something is supposed to happen.

✓ *In my opinion, the subject you **should** talk about is the environment.*

✗ *In my opinion, the subject you ~~will~~ talk about is the environment.*

Choose the correct answer.

1 In my opinion, you *will* / *should* not move schools.
2 If you like the seaside, you *will* / *should* go to the south coast.
3 If we do it that way, it *will* / *should* be a disaster.
4 On this diet, you must eat healthy food, and you *won't* / *shouldn't* drink fizzy drinks.
5 *I'll* / *I should* meet you there if you like.
6 *Will* / *Should* we study everything for the test or just this unit?

UNIT 5

Present simple or present continuous vs. present perfect continuous

Learners sometimes use the present simple or the present continuous when the present perfect continuous is required.
We use the present perfect continuous to talk about how long we have been doing something. We often use it with *for* and *since* and a time period.

✓ *I **have been living** in this house for three years.*

✗ *I ~~live~~ in this house for three years.*

✗ *I ~~am living~~ in this house for three years.*

Correct the following sentences.

1 I try to do that for ages, but I can't manage it.

____

2 How long is Michael learning English?

____

3 I have always been going to work by train, because I live far away.

____

4 His friends laugh every time he is telling that joke – I don't know why.

____

5 I need to fill in your address – where have you been living?

____

6 Since last Wednesday I go to karate lessons.

____

UNIT 6

Future with will

Learners sometimes use the present simple tense when the future tense is required.

✓ *We **will meet** at 9 pm tomorrow.*

✗ *We ~~meet~~ at 9 pm tomorrow.*

Correct the following sentences.

1 We normally will go there every Wednesday.

____

2 I think I will know what you mean.

____

3 So I see you on the 15th.

____

4 I'm sure you want to go there when you see these pictures.

____

5 When I will get home, I'll send you a text.

____

6 Who wins the next football match?

____

UNIT 7

Future forms and time phrases

Learners sometimes use the wrong word order with time phrases.
We put the time phrase after the verbs and object phrases.
✓ *I hope you will come **with me next year.***
✗ *I hope you will come ~~next year with me.~~*

Correct the following sentences.

1 He will look this week at my project.
____
2 I can't straight away help you, but I will as soon as I can.
____
3 I'll do immediately what you've suggested.
____
4 Will you by Friday have it finished?
____
5 I will talk now to him.
____
6 I bet he won't next time do it like that.
____

Question tags

Learners sometimes use the wrong verb in the tag question.
We form question tags by using the same verb if the verb is an auxiliary (*be, have*) or modal verb (*can, will, would*, etc.), but we use *do* with all other verbs.
We use a pronoun which agrees with the subject of the verb, and we keep the tense the same.
✓ *He played the whole game, **didn't he**?*
✗ *He played the whole game, ~~isn't it~~?*

Correct the following question tags.

0 This is a good idea, doesn't it?
This is a good idea, isn't it?
1 He is working on his project, doesn't he?
____
2 We have always wanted to travel, don't we?
____
3 That doesn't sound very interesting, is it?
____
4 You don't finish work at 6 pm, are you?
____
5 It would probably be too far to walk there, isn't it?
____
6 He's driving much too fast on these wet roads, doesn't he?
____

UNIT 8

used to vs. *usually*

Learners sometimes confuse *used to* with *usually*.
We use *used to* to indicate an action that was happening regularly in the past but not now, while *usually* means any action that has happened or is happening regularly.
✓ *When I have some spare time, I **usually** go running in the park.*
✗ *When I have some spare time, I ~~used to~~ go running in the park.*

Complete the sentences with *used to* or *usually*.

0 When I was younger, I *used to* go skiing with my family.
1 If I have time, I _______________ play computer games in the evening.
2 When I was younger I _______________ listen to pop music all the time.
3 They _______________ hang out every Saturday night so that's when I see them.
4 We _______________ buy clothes twice a year, but now that we have extra money we go shopping more often.
5 Now that I go to the tennis club, I _______________ get home late.
6 I _______________ go on camping holidays, but that was a long time ago.

Second conditional tenses

Learners sometimes use the wrong tenses in the clauses of the second conditional.
We form the second conditional by using the past simple tense in the *if* clause, and the *would* form in the main clause.
✓ *If I **knew** what to do, I would do it.*
✗ *If I ~~would know~~ what to do, I would do it.*

Correct the following sentences.

1 If you answered my email, I will be very pleased.
____
2 It would be fantastic if you would come to visit me.
____
3 If I find your mobile, I would bring it on Monday.
____
4 I am very grateful if you could meet me at 11 on Sunday.
____
5 If I broke this vase, my parents will be angry.
____
6 I will love it if you could visit me in the holidays.
____

UNIT 9

Present simple passive vs. past simple passive

Learners sometimes confuse the present simple passive with the past simple passive.
We use the past simple passive to refer to events which took place in the past.
✓ *I* ***was*** *really surprised when I first read the email.*
✗ *I ~~am~~ really surprised when I first read the email.*
We use the present simple passive for events which have started and are still going on now.
✓ *We'll go to Paris in two weeks – the tickets* ***are*** *booked.*
✗ *We'll go to Paris in two weeks – the tickets ~~were~~ booked.*

Correct the following sentences.

1 I always keep shopping until the mall was closed.

____

2 I am born in Britain and have lived here since then.

____

3 I'm proud that my town is chosen as City of Culture.

____

4 The hotel was located in front of the beach, so that will be very convenient.

____

5 Ten minutes later my tent is flooded and I had to leave it because everything was wet.

____

6 I am given a puppy for my last birthday.

____

UNIT 10

Past perfect vs. past simple

Learners often confuse the past perfect with the past simple.
We use the past perfect tense to refer to events which happened at an earlier point in the past, compared with another past event. We use the past simple for an event which occurred generally in the past.
✓ *By the time I got there, he* ***had left.***
✗ *By the time I got there, he ~~left.~~*

Rewrite the sentences using the correct form of the verb in brackets.

0 The trip was awesome because I (dream) about it all my life.
The trip was awesome because I had dreamed about it all my life.

1 Our PE teacher taught us the rules of tennis and we (start) to play.

____

2 I (come) home from school when it happened.

____

3 I didn't give the teacher my homework yesterday because I (leave) my bag at home.

____

4 When we had finished eating and drinking we (go) for a walk in the town centre.

____

5 Do you like these jeans? I (buy) them yesterday.

____

6 The letter was from Brown University – they (accept) me!

____

UNIT 11

say vs. *tell*

Learners often confuse ***say*** **and** ***tell*** **when reporting speech.**
We tell someone (something).
✓ *I* ***told*** *her I was coming to Italy.*
✗ *I ~~said~~ her I was coming to Italy.*
We say something (to someone).
✓ *I* ***said*** *I would go this summer.*
✗ *I ~~told~~ I would go this summer.*

Write a cross (✗) next to the incorrect sentences. Then write the correct sentences.

0 He said me to wait, so I did. ☒
He told me to wait, so I did.

1 My parents told that you can come along. ☐

____

2 She told me to order her a pepperoni pizza. ☐

____

3 As they told, it is a very big sports centre with a lot of facilities. ☐

____

4 I want to say you about this great new computer game. ☐

____

5 I don't know who I can say about this problem. ☐

____

6 She asked me to talk about me and my life. ☐

____

7 Did you say her on what day and at what time she has to be here? ☐

____

8 The customer has made a complaint – he tells that his order hasn't arrived yet. ☐

____

UNIT 12

let vs. make

Learners often confuse when to use *let* and when to use *make*.

We use *let* to indicate that someone is allowed to do something.

✓ *She **let** them have as much ice cream as they wanted.*

✗ *She ~~made~~ them have as much ice cream as they wanted.*

We use *make* to indicate that something or someone is the cause of something.

✓ *The sweet song **made** us all cry.*

✗ *The sweet song ~~let~~ us all cry.*

Choose the correct answer.

1 You can go ahead – I won't *let / make* you wait for me.

2 *Let / Make* me ask you something – do you have any plans for Saturday?

3 Could you *let / make* her know I'll be late?

4 That document really *lets / makes* you think about the problems caused by pollution.

5 They can't *let / make* us stay late if we don't want to.

6 If you help me tidy the house and prepare the food, I'll *let / make* you invite your friends to the party, too.

STUDENT A

UNIT 5, PAGE 54

Student A

1 You're a bit upset. There's a party at the weekend, but your mum says you can't go.
Talk to your friend about the problem.

2 Your friend looks a bit upset. Find out what the problem is and see if you can help.
Why don't you ... ?
You could ...
Can't you ... ?

UNIT 9, PAGE 90

Student A

1 You and some friends are going to the cinema. See if Student B wants to come.

2 Student B invites you to do something with a group of friends. You want to do it.

Does music rock your world? Find out your score!

5–8: Music doesn't rule your world. You like it and you probably listen to it, but it's not so important.

9–11: Music plays an important part in your life, but it isn't the only thing that matters.

12–15: Music is your world and you would find it difficult to live without it. You live, sleep and breathe music.

Key

Q1	A – 1	B – 2	C – 3
Q2	A – 3	B – 2	C – 1
Q3	A – 3	B – 1	C – 2
Q4	A – 1	B – 3	C – 2
Q5	A – 1	B – 2	C – 3

STUDENT B

UNIT 5, PAGE 54

Student B

1 Your friend looks a bit upset. Find out what the problem is and see if you can help.

Why don't you ... ?

You could ...

Can't you ... ?

2 You're a bit upset. It's your mum's birthday tomorrow and you haven't got any money to buy her a present. Talk to your friend about the problem.

UNIT 9, PAGE 90

Student B

1 Student A invites you to do something with a group of friends. You can't do it. Say why you can't.

2 You and some friends are going for a long walk. See if Student A wants to come.